MOTEL CHRONICLES AND HAWK MOON

ff

SAM SHEPARD

Motel Chronicles
& Hawk Moon

faber and faber
LONDON · BOSTON

Motel Chronicles first published in the USA in 1982
by City Lights Books, San Francisco
Hawk Moon first published in the USA in 1981
by Performing Art Journal Publications, New York
First published in Great Britain in 1985
by Faber and Faber Limited
3 Queen Square London WC1 N 3AU
Reprinted 1985 and 1987

Printed in Great Britain by
Redwood Burn Limited, Trowbridge, Wiltshire
All rights reserved

Motel Chronicles © 1982 by Sam Shepard
Hawk Moon © 1973, 1981 by Sam Shepard; © 1981 by Performing
Art Journal Publications

British Library Cataloguing in Publication Data

Shepard, Sam
Motel chronicles; and, Hawk Moon.
I. Title
818'.5409   PS3569.H394

ISBN 0–571–13458–0

MOTEL CHRONICLES
With photographs by Johnny Dark

for my mother
Jane Elaine

never did far away charge so close

César Vallejo

In Rapid City, South Dakota, my mother gave me ice cubes wrapped in napkins to suck on. I was teething then and the ice numbed my gums.

That night we crossed the Badlands. I rode in the shelf behind the back seat of the Plymouth and stared out at the stars. The glass of the window was freezing cold if you touched it.

We stopped on the prairie at a place with huge white plaster dinosaurs standing around in a circle. There was no town. Just these dinosaurs with lights shining up at them from the ground.

My mother carried me around in a brown Army blanket humming a slow tune. I think it was "Peg a' My Heart". She hummed it very softly to herself. Like her thoughts were far away.

We weaved slowly in and out through the dinosaurs. Through their legs. Under their bellies. Circling the Brontosaurus. Staring up at the teeth of Tyrannosaurus Rex. They all had these little blue lights for eyes.

There were no people around. Just us and the dinosaurs.

1/9/80
Homestead Valley, Ca.

His wake-up call came at 5.30 a.m. By now it was a routine. He crossed the grass lot between the motel and the Kettle Pancake House. The Wardrobe Mistress jogged past him in the dark morning light. She was happy to be alone. He could tell by the way she ran. She never seemed that happy sitting around on the set.

He dropped fifteen cents in the red metal box and slid out a copy of the *Austin American Statesman*. He caught a glimpse of the

Soundman and the Dog Trainer leaning over their coffee at each other inside the restaurant. He nodded to them as he entered and took a back booth. He preferred breakfast alone. Just him and the paper. He ordered a plain waffle and coffee. Four Cops were talking Rodeo at the counter behind him. The paper seemed totally devoted to minor stabbings. From the Panhandle to the Gulf, people were getting stabbed: in front of bars, in open fields, in stolen cars, behind pharmacies. He finished his waffle in silence. It left the taste of powdered eggs on his teeth.

He crossed the same plot of grass on his way back to the motel. The same route he'd taken every morning for a month. The tall grass touched him like the whole of Texas. The light was changing fast.

He went through the lobby hoping for mail. His box was empty. The Motel Manager was watching color cartoons in a trance. He could see his Driver waiting for him outside. Pacing.

He slid into the back seat of a grey Cadillac. Two Actors were talking feverishly about Greek Drama. They kept it up for miles. He kept staring silently at the back of the Driver's black cowboy hat. There were three used toothpicks jammed into the hat band. One of those braided horsehair kind of hat bands like the convicts make.

The road seemed extra-treacherous for some reason. Extra-high. Banked in some peculiar way, more like a runway for small prop planes. Farm houses seemed misplaced. Like they belonged in the suburbs or the owners wished they looked like houses that belong in the suburbs. Small attempts at a lawn. A family of white ceramic deer. Bird baths with over-sized metallic green and red Christmas balls sitting in them. Little domestic tokens suddenly ending at an ocean of plowed field.

The Actors kept chattering, using emotional tones in their voices to indicate to each other their deep convictions. At times he felt they were trying harder to convince themselves than each other. The Driver was silent. Relaxed. He was a Wrangler first and a Teamster second. He had absolutely no opinion on the

Greeks nor even the slightest aspiration for one. He kept one
wrist on the top of the wheel while the other one rested. His eyes
looked like they'd plowed a million acres.

They pulled into Uhland. The Honeywagons had taken over
the whole town. Two hundred Extras milled around waiting for
someone to feed them. He searched for his mobile home and
found it parked by a pasture. His costume was waiting. It looked
just like the clothes he had on, like a deflated version of himself.
He switched the clothes he had on for the costume and felt just
the same. Exactly the same. Maybe a little bit stiffer. Cleaner
maybe too. He wondered if he was supposed to be playing
himself. If that's what they hired him for. He sat at the formica
table and stared out at the highway. Two semis passed with the
words HOBBS MIRACLE REVIVAL CRUSADE in bold red
letters painted on the sides. He wondered who the drivers were,
if they believed in God or if they were just driving for others who
believed in God.

All day long he worked the motorcycle behind the camera car.
He kept a constant distance. When the camera car increased
speed he increased the speed of the Kawasaki. He never went
out of focus. Now and then the land would take him out the sides
of his eyes. Broad bands of light shafting down from unbelievable heights, stabbing the horizon like some Italian Religious
Painting. He tried to keep his mind on his business. What the
scene they were shooting was about. Where it fit into the continuity. He was supposed to be riding to kill her? The Star? The
Character? The Woman? The Character he was playing was
supposed to be riding to kill the Character she was playing? He
couldn't take his eyes off the heavy-duty corrugated metal
bumper of the camera car. An Assistant Director held out a small
black electronic blinker with a red light. One blink meant the
camera car was speeding up. Two blinks – slowing down. Three
blinks meant stopping. That was the one he wanted to be sure to
remember. The three blinks one. There was only about a ten-foot
gap of space between the front wheel of the bike and that corru-

gated metal bumper. At sixty miles an hour the meaning of three red blinks was important to remember. But why did he want to kill her? Up 'til now he thought he'd known but suddenly it seemed stupid. Was it just a function of the script or did the Character have a reason? He tried to look grim and determined, staring into the lens. He could see his eyes reflected in the lens. It looked like an act. He dropped it all together. He just rode the bike and forgot about acting. He started enjoying the ride. The Director yelled out to him through a bullhorn: "It looks like you're having too much fun! Look grim and determined! You're riding to kill her!"

The Camera Man kept holding up one, two or three fingers at different intervals. Another code system, this one related to lenses. One finger equaled a wide shot. Two, a medium shot and Three, a tight shot. He tried not to look at the fingers. For him, one finger meant "fairly relaxed"; two equaled "fairly tense"; three – "extremely tense". He wished they hadn't told him what the fingers meant. It didn't do him any good to know. He wasn't doing anything different no matter what lens they were using, no matter how many fingers they held up. So why even tell him? What he needed to know was why did his Character want to kill her Character in the first place? Something about Christ I guess. That was in the script someplace. Something about her being Christ; him thinking she was Christ for some reason. Why would he think she was Christ? He wasn't stupid. The Character wasn't stupid. Why would he think that about her? He remembered the Gospel According to St John where Christ told the Jews: "The reason you don't understand my language is because you don't understand my thought." He was passing the camera car going eighty-five on the Kawasaki. The entire Crew was waving wildly at him to slow down. He didn't see them. The Director threw his hat at the sky. The road looked clean and deadly. He remembered Christ again. What he told the guys who wanted him to prove his miracles in enemy territory: "My time hasn't come yet. For you, it's different. You don't know when your time is coming because you don't know where you come from or where you're going. But me, I know both. And this is not my day to die!"

The Kawasaki spun sideways. The black rubber prop rifle snapped loose from the handlebars and caught him in the neck. He saw the face of the Camera-Car Driver watching him. Apart from him. Dumbly looking. The tallest sky he'd ever seen. The sense of being deep below Heaven. The distance. The wetness of flesh. Metal ripping. People helplessly apart. No sound. The clear sight of Time standing still. Then channeled, isolated sounds of the Land. The Great Tailed Grackle Laughing. The black diamond breast of the Meadow Lark. Beating. Dancing between the furrows. Leafless Live Oak.

Suddenly he appeared to himself. He caught himself in a flash. There was no more doubt who the Character was.

3/79
Shiner, Texas

I remember trying to imitate Burt Lancaster's smile after I saw him and Gary Cooper in *Vera Cruz*. For days I practiced in the back yard. Weaving through the tomato plants. Sneering. Grinning that grin. Sliding my upper lip up over my teeth. After a few days of practice I tried it out on the girls at school. They didn't seem to notice. I broadened my interpretation until I started getting strange reactions from the other kids. They would look straight at my teeth and a fear would creep into their eyes. I'd forgotten how bad my teeth were. How one of the front ones was dead and brown and overlapped the broken one right next to it. I'd actually come to believe I was in possession of a full head of perfect pearly Burt Lancaster-type teeth. I didn't want to scare anyone so I stopped grinning after that. I only did it in private. Pretty soon even that faded. I returned to my empty face.

25/4/81
Homestead Valley, Ca.

He changed the canaries
Fed the Mule
Stood transfixed for ½ an hour

Every morning
He changed the canaries
Fed the Mule
And stood transfixed for ½ an hour

He never planned on standing transfixed for ½ an hour
It just happened
Every morning

Maybe it was the pause in finishing feeding the Mule
The momentum running down

There seemed to be a natural momentum
From changing the canaries
To feeding the Mule

There was never any problem
Moving from the canaries
To the Mule

It just happened
Every morning

It was the pause
After feeding the Mule
That stunned him

A Giant Pause

He even knew what the next thing was
He knew it very clearly

He knew the next thing was feeding himself
After feeding the Mule

But he couldn't move

He stood transfixed for ½ an hour
Staring at the desert

Sometimes staring at his bottle house

Sometimes staring at the well pump

It depended on which direction he happened to be facing
When the transfixion struck him

It got to the point where he looked forward
To standing transfixed for ½ an hour

It was the high point of his morning

Change the canaries
Feed the Mule
Stand transfixed for ½ an hour

15/1/80
Homestead Valley, Ca.

Evidently I walk in my sleep. They find me standing at the end of
the hallway by the hibiscus-flowered wallpaper, mumbling to
myself. They say the words are unintelligible and when they
shake me I shut up. They lead me by the shoulder back to bed
and I fall asleep and don't walk again the whole rest of the night.

When they tell me the next morning how they'd found me like this I'm filled with a kind of warm glow. My spine buzzes. I smile uncontrollably and my Dad says: "It's not funny." But he has a smile too when he says it and that makes me smile even more uncontrollably.

One night I walked into the bathroom in my sleep and climbed into the empty white tub. They found me asleep in there on my side. Their reaction to this was more severe than when they'd found me at the end of the hallway. A slightly worried tone crept into their voices. For some reason they felt climbing into the bathtub was too bizarre. A little crazy maybe. Even though (when I was much younger) my mother had often bedded me down in bathtubs all over Idaho while my Dad was away in the Air Force dropping bombs on Italy and there was only one narrow bed in the motels.

I don't know why my imaginings of these nightly sojourns were so compelling to me but I began to look forward to the morning explanations by my parents of where they'd found me the night before. Where had I traveled? Would they have found me on the ceiling this time? Curled up inside the fireplace? I couldn't stand the fact that I was missing out on these unconscious encounters so I invented a brave scheme: I would *pretend* I was sleep-walking. I would keep my eyes closed tightly and sort of stumble down the hallway, bumping into walls, breathing deeply and maybe make a little low sound so they'd be sure to hear me. It took me hours to work up enough guts to follow through with this plan because I knew if I failed they'd probably think all the other times had been faked and there'd be no way of telling what their reaction would be to that.

I waited up until I was sure they were both in bed. I could hear them giggling, which meant they were probably engaging in foreplay. I swung out of bed with my eyes closed and guided myself to the hallway – past the snarling Tiger painted on silk, brought back by my Dad from the Philippines; past the portrait of a train conductor painted by my Grandfather; past the pink

Hibiscus flowers glowing in the light from the bathroom. Halfway down the hallway I could hear them stop giggling. My heart crashed. I could smell the wallpaper. I could hear them whispering. This was it! This is what it must've been like all those other nights but this time I was here for it. The situation seemed deeply dangerous. My pretending demanded conviction. There was no going back. I steadily stumbled toward the end of the hallway. I squeezed my eyes tighter. Swung my arms looser. I could feel them watching me through the crack of their bedroom door. They were buying it so far. I was pulling off the illusion! Then, suddenly I realized the end of the hallway was almost upon me. Their bedroom door. I would reach the end of the hallway and there'd be no place to go. Would I just stand there snoring? Would I hit the wall, turn around and head back to my bedroom like some kind of bumper-car toy? Would I lie down and mumble? Would I keep walking in place with my nose pressed to the wallpaper? In a quick flash of inspiration I remembered the phone. The big black phone at the end of the hallway sitting on a small round table. I fumbled for the receiver and picked it up, purposely putting the wrong end to my ear. I began mumbling to an imaginary being on the other end. That was all it took. The game was up. They burst from the bedroom, grabbed me firmly by the shoulders and shook me. I popped my eyes open with a broad display of shock and amazement but it didn't work. I was swept down the hallway and plopped into bed. "Now stay in bed!" is what they said. "Don't get out of bed again. It's not a bit funny." Humor was the furthest thing from my mind. It wasn't to make them laugh. It was only for the thrill of having a relationship with them outside the ordinary. A different kind of encounter. Now it was over. Now it was just a humiliating silence lying in the dark.

They closed their bedroom door and I couldn't even hear them. My kid sister rolled over in the bunk bed above me. She mumbled something in her sleep. She'd just learned to talk. I spoke something back to her but she didn't answer. The guy next

door turned on his sprinkler system. I could hear him singing to
his roses.

13/10/80
LA, Ca.

3:30 a.m.

is it a rooster
or some woman screaming in the distance

is it black sky
or about to turn deep blue

is it a motel room
or someone's house

is it the body of me alive
or dead

is it Texas
or West Berlin

what time is it
anyway

what thoughts
can I call allies

I pray for a break
from all thought

a clean break
in blank space

let me hit the road
empty-headed

just once

I'm not begging

I'm not getting down on my knees

I'm in no condition to fight

9/12/80
Fredericksburg, Texas

He washed his red shirt in the sink. Laid a motel towel on the floor. Laid the shirt on the towel. As he smoothed the sleeves and crossed them on the belly of the shirt he thought of his own death. Of how they might cross his arms just like the sleeves on his own dead belly. He laid a second towel on top of the red shirt so the shirt was sandwiched then walked on top of the towel with his bare feet, making tight mincing steps, squeezing the water out. This was something he'd picked up from his mother. He'd seen her do this with her own bare feet on top of blue fuzzy sweaters with small synthetic shells for buttons. He'd seen her toes curl. Watched water squish out faintly bluer than water. Bleeding from dye. He thought of her feet and pictured them so vividly that his whole mother appeared before him.

He peeled off the top towel, lifted the shirt like a hide and hung it. The red shirt waved in the wind of the air-conditioner. He thought it was a flag for a second. He thought it might be a Ghost Shirt. He turned to the window for no reason. He was forty-some-miles from Austin. Outside, Chicano maids in pink sweaters pushed laundry carts down cement corridors speaking Spanish softly. He could hear they were related by blood.

He moved to the bed. Stared at the cover of a book: *Views of Los Angeles – 125 Black and White Photographs Contrasting the Past with the Present*. He rolled on the bed. Listened to the toilet. Listened to the bones in his back. Listened to her screaming in the back of his head. Thought he heard her screaming. Thought for sure he heard her speaking voice. (She couldn't achieve an orgasm is what it was. So she would imitate her idea of the sounds of an ultimate orgasm. Every time she repeated it she would try to top the last imitation until finally she sounded more like she was being murdered than loved.)

He jumped up. Ran out to the bottom of the steel steps. Past the Ice Machine. Past two skinny cats. Felt something running through him. Like ice. Like the way the Ice Machine made this thought run through him. He stopped. Just short of his truck. Stains of chewing tobacco sprayed on the door in the patterns forced by highway wind made his stomach sink. His own stains. Made him think he was maybe losing his grip. He ran back to the room. Grabbed a small towel. Soaked it in hot water. Rang it out. Felt the heat through his hands. Just barely burning. Turned his head from his hands like the hurt from the heat was much bigger. A much bigger burn running deeper than skin. He ran back down. Began wiping the door of his truck with a fury. Some bizarre fear that he might get caught with an ugly truck. Even by strangers.

Slowly this wiping was changing his mind. He felt this wiping was catching him up to himself. Very slowly. He finished the door. Moved on to the windows. Noticed the gas stains surrounding the gas cap. Moved on to those then figured he'd wipe the whole truck. This total commitment to wiping was bringing him home. The towel was black. People with luggage were standing there watching. He turned to them. They disappeared. The truck had turned startling silver.

He tossed the black towel with the form he used to use for High School jump-shots at the top of the key. As the towel arced toward the orange steel disposal box the thought came in that if he missed, something very bad would happen very soon. He didn't miss.

He got in the truck and sat for a long time without moving. He watched a green Sports Page blow across a vacant lot. Watched it catch on short sticker weeds then free itself and blow into a barbed-wire fence. Three Robins watched it too. He'd never seen Robins in this kind of weather. It troubled him deeply the way their feathers blew and they weren't even flying.

When it got dark he left the truck and checked his box in the lobby. A postcard from Muskogee showing the Post Office and Federal Court House in faded yellow. On the back in black scrawl it read: "Darling, I got the report back from the doctor and he said, it's best I don't see you no more." That was it. No signature. Nothing. He poked his head into the motel bar, hoping to find Billy Wells. A fat woman holding a Chihuahua in her lap was sitting alone with a Whiskey Sour. She waved to him as though she knew him. He didn't wave back.

He carried the postcard outside to the pool. The glare off the water made his eyes blink so he shut them. He crossed the dead grass and heard a garden hose spraying cement. He opened his eyes. A Mexican man was waving him across a patch of wet cement and holding the hose to one side. As he moved across, the man sprayed his boots and laughed. He laughed back but thought it was a dumb joke.

He left the door of his room open. Placed the postcard in the frame of the mirror. Washed his face in the sink. Moved to the window wiping his face with a T-shirt. A wind invaded the room through the open door. The postcard fell from the mirror. A waiter carried a salad wrapped in cellophane past his window. A form burst through the door. A man the size of a train. Two fists blasted him in the shoulders. Then one to the side of his head. He went down. He hit the air conditioner with his knee. His nose hit the edge of a glass table. He was kicked once in the back. The form spoke: "You ever mess with Virgie agin, I'll kill ya!"

He just lay there for a long time. Right where he fell. Listened.

Not afraid the form would return. Just listened to how things were with him. He stared up at his red shirt still dripping from the hanger. He heard it dripping. He knew it must have been dripping like that for days. Marking time. Phone rang. He couldn't reach it. He didn't want to reach it. It rang for a long time. Someone walked past his open door. "Phone's ringing," they said as they passed. Phone stopped. He didn't even imagine who it was on the other end. He just saw it as a phone. Ringing. Black phone. He stayed there through the night. Right where he'd fell.

3/79
San Marcos, Texas

He prowled the pool
Of the Holiday Inn
And felt a fit of uselessness

The sight of a pool
At midnight
In Texas

Poor Texas
Carved into
Like all the rest

3/79
San Marcos, Texas

The first time I ran away from school I was ten. Two older guys talked me into it. They were brothers and they'd both been in and out of Juvenile Hall five times. They told me it would just be like taking a short vacation. So I went. We stole three bikes out of a back yard and took off for the Arroyo Seco. The bike I stole was too big for me so I could never sit up on the seat all the way. I pedaled standing.

We hid the bikes in a stand of Eucalyptus trees at the edge of the Arroyo and went down to the creek. We caught Crawdads with marshmallow bait then tore the shells off them and used

25

their meat to catch more Crawdads. When lunch time came I had to share my lunch with the brothers because they'd forgotten to bring theirs. I spread the contents of the paper bag out on a big flat rock. A carrot wrapped in wax paper with a rubber band around it. A meatloaf sandwich. A melted bag of M and Ms. They ate the M and Ms first. Tore the package open and licked the chocolate off the paper. They offered me a lick but I declined. I didn't eat any of the meatloaf sandwich either. I always hated meatloaf. Especially cold and between bread.

The rest of the afternoon we climbed around in the hills looking for snakes until one of them got the idea of lowering our bikes down into the aqueduct and riding along the dry bed until we reached Los Angeles. I said "yes" to everything even though I suspected LA was at least a hundred miles away. The only other time I'd ever been to Los Angeles was when my Aunt took me to the Farmer's Market in her '45 Dodge to look at the Myna birds. I must have been six then.

I climbed the chain-link barrier fence while the two brothers took the tension out of the barb-wire strands at the top. Enough so I could straddle the fence, get one foot on the concrete wall of the aqueduct and drop some ten or twelve feet to the bottom. Then they lowered the bikes down to me, suspended on their belts. We rode for miles down this giant corridor of cement, the wheels of our bikes bumping over the brown lines of caulking used to seal the seams. Except for those seams it was the smoothest, flattest surface I'd ever ridden a bike on.

We rode past red shotgun shells faded by the sun, dead opossums, beer cans, Walnut shells, Carob pods, a Raccoon with two babies, pages out of porno magazines, hunks of rope, inner tubes, hub caps, bottle caps, dried-up Sage plants, boards with nails, stumps, roots, smashed glass, yellow golf balls with red stripes, a lug wrench, women's underwear, tennis shoes, dried-up socks, a dead dog, mice, Dragon Flies screwing in mid-air, shriveled-up frogs with their eyes popped out. We rode for miles until we came to a part that was all enclosed like a big long tunnel

and we couldn't see light at the other end. We stopped our bikes
and stared through the mouth of that tunnel and I could tell they
were just as scared as I was even though they were older. It was
already starting to get dark and the prospect of getting stuck in
there at night, not knowing how long the thing was or what town
we'd come out in or how in the hell we were going to climb back
out once we came to the end of it had us all wishing we were back
home. None of us said we wished that but I could feel it passing
between us.

I don't remember how the decision was made but we pushed
off straight ahead into it. The floor was concave and slick with
moss, causing the wheels to slip sideways. Sometimes our feet
came down ankle-deep in sludge and black mud and we ended
up having to walk the bikes through most of it. We kept making
sounds to each other just to keep track of where we were as the
light disappeared behind us. We started out trying to scare each
other with weird noises but gave it up because the echoes were
truly terrifying. I kept having visions of Los Angeles appearing
suddenly at the other end of the tunnel. It would just pop up at
us, all blinking with lights and movement and life. Sometimes it
would appear like I'd seen it in postcards. (Palm Trees set against
a background of snowy mountains with orange groves sprawling
beneath them. The Train Station with a burro standing in front of
it, harnessed to a cart.) But it didn't come. For hours it didn't
come. And my feet were wet. And I forgot what the two brothers
even looked like anymore. I kept having terrible thoughts about
home. About what would happen when I finally got back. In the
blackness I pictured our house. The red awning. The garage
door. The strip of lawn down the center of the driveway. The
Pyracantha berries. The Robins that ate them. Close-ups of the
Robin's beak guzzling red berries. So close I could see little
dribbles of dirt from wet lawns where he'd been pulling out
worms. I couldn't stop these pictures. (Me walking to school. The
chubby old Crossing Guard at the corner with his round wooden
sign that read STOP in red letters. The dirt playground. Porcelain

27

water fountains with silver knobs dribbling. The face of the kid I hit in the stomach for no reason. Little traces of mayonnaise around his lips.) I had the feeling these pictures would drown me. I wondered what the two brothers were thinking but I never asked them.

It was night when we reached the end and it wasn't Los Angeles either. Huge Sycamore trees with hazy orange street lights loomed over our heads. We could hear the sound of a freeway. Periodic whooshing of trucks. We hauled ourselves out by climbing on each other's shoulders and hooking the belts to the top of the fence. The oldest brother said he recognized the town we were in. He said it was Sierra Madre and he had an Uncle who lived pretty close by. We pedaled to his Uncle's house and we weren't talking to each other at that point. There was nothing to say.

His Uncle lived in a small three-room house with several men sitting around the front room drinking beer and watching the Lone Ranger on TV. Nobody seemed surprised to see us. They acted like this had happened a lot before. A woman was making a big pot of spaghetti in the kitchen and she gave us each a paper plate and told us to wait for the meat sauce to heat up. We sat on the floor at the feet of the men in the front room and watched the Lone Ranger and ate spaghetti. That was the first time I'd ever seen TV because we didn't have one at home. (My Dad said we didn't need one.) I liked the Lone Ranger a lot. Especially the music when he galloped on Silver and reared up waving his hat at a woman holding a baby.

We were finally caught later that night by a squad car on a bridge in South Pasadena. The cops acted like we were adults. They had that kind of serious tone: "Where did you get these bikes? What are your names? Where do you live? Do you know what time it is?" Stuff like that. They radioed our parents and confiscated the bikes. My mother showed up and drove me back, explaining how my Dad was so pissed off that he wouldn't come because he was afraid he'd kill me. She kept saying, "Now you've got a Police Record. You'll have that the rest of your life."

I got whipped three times with the buckle-end of my Dad's belt. Three times. That was it. Then he left the house. He never said a word.

I lay in bed listening to my mother ironing in the kitchen. I pictured her ironing. The hiss of steam. The sprinkle bottle she used to wet my Dad's shirts. I pictured her face staring down at the shirt as her arm moved back and forth in a steady tempo.

13/8/80
Homestead Valley, Ca.

my Mom carried a .45 for a while
me on one hip
the pistol on the other
I lived in a community of women
pilots' wives
quonset huts
it rained all the time

the wives were edgy
without their men
Japanese swarmed through the jungle
stole wet laundry off the lines
the women fired at the least provocation
sometimes at each other's shadows

my Mom and I were fired on once
by her best friend
the bullets left big ragged holes
through the tin walls

later I found a Japanese skull
out by the reservoir
ants were crawling
out of a bullet hole
right through the temple

26/12/81
Homestead Valley, Ca.

The truck disappeared in a place called Plains. The streets were solid brick. Low-riders cruised in Mavericks. There was incomprehensible traffic as he searched for motels. He found one, advertising itself as "A Touch of Velvet – Luxury Rooms". He felt he deserved a little velvet. To be touched by velvet was exactly what he craved. That velvet might be a refuge from the road.

He took the most expensive room without caring if he got his money's worth. The room had a synthetic smell that he couldn't put his finger on. Probably rug-cleaning fluids. The walls were red velvet flocked. The bed spreads were red velvet. The chairs were red velvet. The rug was red velvet. The sink was red. The curtains were red. All the reds were matching red. There was no red less red than another red or more red than the red next to it. The room was red velvet vengeance. He made himself to home.

He flipped on the TV. A Preacher was preaching in sign language. He noticed the sign for "Jesus" was alternately tapping the palms of each hand with the middle finger, denoting the nails of the crucifixion. He turned the sound off and watched the hands of the Preacher. He thought he saw language leaping across the room. ("And not one of his bones shall be broken.")

He fell asleep in the shower, standing up. He dreamed of a man he'd known as a boy. Tied to a Sycamore tree. Burned for no reason. The tree remained with a black gash that finally closed, revealing nothing but pink bark. Clean as a baby's chin. When he awoke he could still see the man. He thought it was raining on his head. And the man was floating. And the ashes of the body of the man were running down his face.

("And not one of his bones shall be broken.")

3/79
Plains, Texas

31

Down in the bottom of the bottom land
you can hear the old man
crying out for "Mama!"
hanging sideways off his cot
one arm hanging

You can hear the young gun
dying for a girl
while the semis pile by

Down here in the very bottom of the low land
in the rockabilly bottle club
Lou-Ann bites the mike
spits blues back
through the long wet night

25/10/80
Austin, Texas

Black cloud shadows
on the Orocopia Mountains

Gigantic Date Palms
brown bags protecting their fruit

Alfalfa trucks
orange trucks filled with tires

Tangerine groves
ladders leaning on their trunks

Roofless stone foundations
made from river rock

Single burned Palm
nothing around it burned

Giant chunks of truck tires
frying on the road

Trailered racing boat
solid chrome pipes

Dust blows
all over Blythe

14/10/80
Coachella, Ca.

Me and Tim Ford stole a car once in San Bernardino. One of those early Austin Healeys with red leather tuck and roll and wire wheels. It was just sitting there with the keys in it behind an A and W Root Beer Stand.

At first we were just going to drive it around for a while then leave it on the other side of town but we ended up heading for Mexico instead. Tim had this idea that we needed to get some false ID so we could drink in bars and buy beer in liquor stores without getting hassled. He said he knew about this guy in Tijuana who forged the date of birth on your driver's license and that there was no way of telling it from the real thing. He said it was cheap too.

I can't remember a car that was as much fun to drive as that Austin Healey. It growled. It responded like an animal to every cue. It flashed through down-shifts, double-clutching, speed-shifts – anything you could throw at it. It cornered like a Panther. There was no way you could turn it over.

33

The two of us began taking on the personalities of Austin Healey owners. We opened our shirts and let the wind beat our chests. We traded off using the pair of dark glasses we found in the glove compartment. (They were red-rimmed with little green rhinestones on the corners.) We slip-streamed women on the highway and pulled up close enough to grab their door handles and hear them scream. When we stopped at a restaurant we'd get a booth by the window so we could stare out at the car. The cat-mouth grill work. We dreamed of racing it across Europe and started using jargon like "Pit Stop" and "Team Rally" for those within earshot. We loved that Healey like we were its true owners.

We spent all day in Tijuana waiting for the guy to develop the pictures he took of us for the phony ID. He was a silent, sullen little man in a stained grey sweater. We kept wandering around town and returning to his office every half hour. He would crack his door open and wave us away with quick flicks of his hands, like we were beggars or something. I had the feeling that false ID was the least of his illegal operations. It turned out to be worth the wait though. The new licenses were impeccable and passed the test at the border when the cops asked us to take them out of our wallets.

We drank up a storm in San Diego, flaunting our new cards at every bartender in town. We bought four bottles of Ripple Wine for the trip back home. We didn't even stop to get sick, we just puked into the wind and turned the radio up.

11/9/80
San Francisco, Ca.

34

I knew a guitar player who called the radio "friendly". He felt a kinship not with the music so much as with the radio's voice. Its synthetic quality. Its voice as distinct from the voices coming through it. Its ability to transmit the illusion of people at a great distance. He slept with the radio. He talked to the radio. He disagreed with the radio. He believed in a Faraway Radio Land. He believed he would never find this land so he reconciled himself to listening to it only. He believed he'd been banned from the Radio Land and was doomed to prowl the air waves forever, seeking some magic channel that would reinstate him to his long-lost heritage.

22/12/79
Homestead Valley, Ca.

35

King Solomon's Mines was the movie that most haunted me as a kid. I've never seen it since then but images from it still remain. Watusi warriors with red clay stripes down their noses. Raised black welts studding their chests. Teeth filed down to needle points. Lions ripping someone's arm off. Flies landing on someone's lip and the lip not moving. Torches in caves. Blue jewels surrounded by skulls. That English actor guy half scared to death.

The Rialto Theatre was dark and musky in the middle of day and I entered the world of the movie so completely that the theatre became a part of its landscape. The trip to get popcorn up the black aisle with the sound track booming and the kids squealing in their seats was all part of the plot. I was in the cave of King Solomon at the candy counter. The "Ju-Ju-Bees" were jewels. The ushers were jungle trees. Cheetahs roamed through the bathroom.

I breathed African dust for days afterwards in a town of solid white folk.

1/9/80
Homestead Valley, Ca.

when I encountered the Star's stand-in
as the elevator doors slid open
and I was stepping out
as she was stepping in
at 4 a.m.
and I saw that she was radically stoned
I asked her what on
she said 6 Valium and White Wine
because this was our last day of shooting
so she thought she'd celebrate
by balling someone on the crew
and getting zipped
since this was her home town
and she'd be staying right here
while we'd be moving on
and the agony of being just a local stand-in
left behind
in a town she ached to be out of
was bearing down on her now
with real force
and it made me suddenly re-ashamed
of being an actor in a movie
at all
and provoking such stupid illusions
so I took her to my room
with no designs on her body
at all
and she was desperately disappointed
tried to throw herself out my window
I said look it's not worth it
it's just a dumb movie
she said it's not as dumb as life

1/11/81
Seattle, Wa.

37

people here
have become
the people
they're pretending to be

27/7/81
Los Angeles, Ca.

On the train that I love so much. The train they named and re-named: first, according to the terrain it crossed, then, later, to jibe with a corporate sense of anonymity. The train remains the same. And all the same feelings swell up in me on this train. Same wonders. Same heart-breaking hunger for the land out the window. I'd live on a train if someone gave me one.

On this same train I'm sitting down in the diner. Scanning. Pretending to read the menu. A Tuesday Weld-type-of-blonde girl, maybe fifteen, in bare feet is reading a thick green book and dawdling with a salad. She keeps looking straight at me then back to the book. I can't take my eyes off her feet. It's her feet that remind me of Tuesday Weld more than her hair. It's her feet that take me back to an early TV Talk Show where Tuesday Weld appeared in bare feet and a full skirt and the interviewer (I think it was David Susskind) spent the whole time putting her down for having bare feet on his show and how this was a strong indic-ation of her neurotic immaturity and need for attention. I fell in love with Tuesday Weld on that show. I thought she was the Marlon Brando of women.

This girl keeps staring at me over her thick green book and I'm getting all constricted around the throat. She's wearing one of those blue stretchy kind of tops with no straps. The kind you just pull straight down and everything becomes instantly available. She seems to be taking a long time to finish her salad.

I move over to her table and ask her what she's reading.

"The History of American Suicide," she says.

I say, "Are you a student of Suicide?"

She says, "No."

I say, "Oh."

One thing leads to another and we wind up in her stateroom. She's only fifteen, I'm thinking. I'm only nineteen. Fifteen and nineteen. That means when I was four, she was nowhere. She says she's a Mormon. She says her Daddy's picking her up in Salt Lake. (*I'm picturing her Daddy in a broad-brimmed black hat, black suit, black string tie, seated in a buggy behind a black mule with a whip in one hand, waiting at the train station. Sea gulls slowly circling above his head.*)

She unfolds the bed from the wall. She thinks it's a joke. The bed falls into place leaving no room to stand. The train jerks. Her top comes down even easier than I imagined. She tells me she can't "do" and I've never heard this expression before so I say, "Do what?" We "do" all the way from Winnemucca through the Great Salt Lake Desert. It's a lot like crossing the ocean at night. A sea train. Salt glows white through the window. She says she'll never be able to face her boyfriend again.

When the train pulls into Salt Lake I watch her leap from the metal steps of the coach straight through a cloud of steam. I hear her bare feet hit the gravel but she's gone. There's a strong smell of steel in the air. Lights from the station platform. Red Caps pushing baggage carts. The steam thins out and a street appears in the distance. I have an itch to follow the street. Just abandon ship and follow her, but she's nowhere in sight. "Tuesday!" I yell out to the Salt Lake City night. "Tuesday, don't leave me!"

Back in my seat, the train rolls. I suddenly start having vivid premonitions that she'll spill the beans to her Daddy. I expect retaliation at every stop. Doors bursting open. (*Her Daddy has taken on a Sterling Hayden face now and carries a twelve-gauge shotgun. I'm terrified the train will stop in some remote outpost and the conductor will hand me over to the vindictive father. I'll be carried into the desert and*

39

beheaded. I'll be mutilated like Osiris and this blonde little Isis will come searching for my parts. Piecing me back together. It will take her years to find all my members and still my most private organs will have escaped her, floating down the Colorado River deep into Mexico. She'll follow the river, mourning my fractured corpse. Holding my severed head up to the moon and moaning as she floats. The sound of her lament will fill the Grand Canyon.)

At 1.30 a.m. I get off in Missouri. I'm due for Chicago in the morning but I can't stand to ride it out. At least on foot I'll have a chance. I find a phone booth by a corn field and call Illinois collect. My Grandmother answers. She's not glad to hear from me. She's not glad to be paying for this call. She can't picture where I am or why I'm calling. "I'm in a phone booth by a corn field in Missouri. Right near the Mississippi." She can't figure it out. I haven't seen her for seven years or even written her a letter. "I'm coming in to see you tomorrow. How's Grandpa?" She asks me if I realize what time it is. "Yeah, I'm sorry, Grandma, but I had to get off the train. I was afraid for my life."

I take a Greyhound into Chicago then hitch out to the country. The farm looks abandoned. A small stand of dried-up corn stalks by the house with dead crows that my Grandfather's shot hanging by their necks, tied with red rubber bands so they bounce slightly when the wind hits them. My Grandpa's theory is that they function as scarecrows to the living crows.

My Grandpa sits exactly as he's always sat – in a hole of his sofa wrapped in crocheted blankets facing the TV. He's like a skeleton now. He likes the Hamm's Beer commercials. "The Land of Sky Blue Waters." The little cartoon Beaver that jumps around on top of the waterfall and sings the jingle. He thinks Truman was our greatest President and writes political rebuffs to the Chicago papers, signing them "Plain Dirt Farmer". He predicts "a Nigger in the White House" by 1970. He's a staunch fan of the Chicago Cubs. He tells me I never should have abandoned baseball. "You could've had a career in the Majors," he says. "Not a bad life. Gettin' paid to play ball." He smokes and drinks continuously and spits blood into a stand-up brass ash tray like you see in the lobbies of old hotels. Sometimes he coughs so violently that his whole body doubles over and he can't catch his breath for a long long time. His world is circumscribed around the sofa. Everything he needs is within a three-foot reach. The TV is only on for the baseball. When the game ends my Grandmother comes in and turns it off. She does it right on cue. She can hear when the game ends from any room in the house. She has great ears.

When everyone's asleep I wander around in the room upstairs staring at all the photographs of my Uncles. The Uncle who died in a motel room on his wedding night. His wife who died with him. The Uncle who lost a leg at the age of ten. The Uncle who married into the Chicago Mafia. The Uncle who cut timber in the Great North Woods. The Uncle who drove for Bekins. The Uncle who raised Springer Spaniels. All the Uncles who carry the bones of my Grandpa's face.

I fall back on the bed. "Fifteen and nineteen," I'm thinking. "Fifteen and nineteen." A train whistles way off. Cicadas buzz. I can still hear her feet hit the gravel.

24/9/80
San Francisco, Ca.

Luck
is falling
on the left side
of Chance

Luck
is falling
past my head

Luck
is crashing
through the trees

everyone's complaining

27/7/81
San Fernando Valley

His feet were sweating in the night. He could feel the presence of the automatic pistol, of cattle, of barbed wire, of dice, of riding the night range without a flashlight, of bars plunged into prairie night.

He turned off all the lights in the room and lay on the floor between the two beds. His feet were sweating. He punched the switch of the Realistic tape machine and Stevie Wonder answered the darkness: "Songs in the Key of Life."

He watched an Apache Sand Painting appear on the wall out of nowhere. Colors from the land: pale orange sand, chocolate topsoil, pale blue like a tear.

He could see the giant of Abalone shimmer off the pistol stock. Threads of rosy light. Spinning. He could see his own heart.

He could feel the demonic attachment of a man for his only woman.

3/79
San Marcos, Texas

My name came down through seven generations of men with the same name each naming the first son the same name as the father then the mothers nicknaming the sons so as not to confuse them with the fathers when hearing their names called in the open air while working side by side in the waist-high wheat.

The sons came to believe their names were the nicknames they heard floating across these fields and answered to these names building ideas of who they were around the sound never dreaming their real legal name was lying in wait for them written on some paper in Chicago and that name would be the name they'd prefix with "Mr" and that name would be the name they'd die with.

2/5/80
Homestead Valley, Ca.

He picks me up every morning in his red pickup. It's always too early. I'm always rushing to get the sheep fed at the last minute. I'm never glad to go to work.

We always drive through the same fields. In the dark. Past the same cattle. Their white faces glow. Almost always we see the same red coyote trotting across the pasture in the rut he's made through repetition. He points and says, "Look, there he is again!" He says that every time we see him.

I strip the stalls right down to the concrete floor. My eyes burn from horse piss. My hands burn from lime. The light is just coming up through the Deodar Pines.

They're breeding two mares this morning and they want me to help wash down the stallion. They say it's time I learn how to do this. We sponge the stallion's penis with soapy water. It must be a yard long at least. He strikes out at us so we rig him into a Scotch hobble and put a twitch on his lip. He keeps acting like he

43

might throw himself down so we blindfold him with burlap and twist his ear. He finally settles.

At lunch I try to eat by myself but there's this daughter of the owner who comes around and always tries to engage me in conversation. She wears those English jodhpur kind of pants and sometimes carries a short whip that she taps very gently on her knee bone. I think she's seen *National Velvet* too many times.

At night he drives me back and I just barely have enough time to feed the sheep again before it gets pitch black. When I'm done I almost never want to go up to the house for supper. Sometimes I just stand outside and watch my family moving around inside the house. I stand there a long time sometimes. They don't know that I watch them.

22/9/80
San Francisco, Ca.

He tried to boost an absolutely worthless print of a Cottonwood Tree stranded in a dry desert basin from the Chateau Marmont Hotel on Sunset Boulevard.

They caught him with it in the parking lot, cramming it into the bed of his pickup.

When they asked him why, he told them he wasn't sure why. He told them it gave him this feeling.

He told them he saw himself inside this picture lying on his back underneath the Cottonwood.

He said he recognized the tree from an old dream and that the dream was based on a real tree he dimly remembered from a long time ago in his childhood.

He remembered lying down underneath this tree and staring up through the silver leaves.

He remembered voices from those leaves but he couldn't remember what the voices said or who they belonged to.

He told them he was hoping the picture would bring the whole thing back.

25/7/81
Hollywood, Ca.

She'd written Chicago for the details of my birth. I told her I wasn't born in Chicago, that I was born way out in the boondocks somewhere. Somewhere obscure. (Trying to make a big impression.) One way or another she tracked down the very hospital where the event took place. She was determined. She said she had a chart in mind. Something on paper linking me to the movements of the planets. She asked all kinds of questions in her letter to the Head Nurse and the Head Nurse supplied her with all kinds of answers. (All of them fictitious as far as I could tell.) For example, the exact time of my birth, according to this Head Nurse, was three in the afternoon on the fifth of November, 1943. ("Guy Fawkes Day", where the kids in England make these dummy dolls and sit in front of stores saying, "Penny for the Guy.") But I have verification from other sources (not my Mother) that it was something like 2.47 a.m. which puts me in the wee hours of the freezing morning. It was a barren room with a white tile floor and two windows overlooking Lake Michigan, which at that time of year was smothered in mammoth green icebergs. There was no traffic on the streets below and the town was dark due to the wartime curfew.

I plunged into the world head first and, although covered with blood, my attitude was very friendly. I was not a mean person then. These anonymous sources went on to say that my general thrust at that time was only to see the ice. I lurched off the bed and dragged my pudgy body toward those two windows. My mother had fallen unconscious from the ordeal and there was no nurse in attendance so I took full advantage of my new mobility in the outside. I found that my arms were much stronger than the bottom half of me. I could pull everything behind me. I knew I wasn't a colt. That I wouldn't be standing up on those legs for quite some months to come. I knew I wasn't a frog or a bird for sure. So I just dragged the rest of me straight toward those windows.

When I reached the wall I began to get my first taste of what it's like to suffer. The windows were directly overhead but too high to reach in my condition. Pale green light poured through them, casting a double beam on my unconscious mother across the room. I watched her body. I knew I'd come from her body but I wasn't sure how. I knew I was away from her body now. Separate. The wall was chocolate brown. I heard a humming which turned out to be warplanes. B–29s. I felt a tremendous panic suddenly. I was between these two worlds. The world I'd left behind and this new one. I had no idea where to turn.

At this point the mysterious witnesses to my birth claim they lost track of my progress. They had assumed everything was hunky-dory with me so they took off across the green icebergs in the direction of Lake Erie.

My girl friend drew up her chart according to the bogus data she'd obtained from the Head Nurse. She told me that I had an interesting but very difficult life ahead of me and that my Saturn was lined up in exactly the same position as Goethe's. I didn't ask her for any further details. She looked so sweet and innocent.

3/7/81
Cotati, Ca.

Now lemme get this straight

You say
You're tortured because you can't write
Or
You can't write because you're tortured

You say
These times have made you cynical
Or
These times confirm your cynicism

Now lemme say one thing
I'd rather rope steers
Than talk politics with you

I'd rather get skunk drunk
Under a goose-neck trailer

Your despair is more boring
Than *The Merv Griffin Show*

Your sniveling whine
Your dime-a-dozen solutions to crime

Get off your tail and cook
Do time
Anything
But don't burn mine

2/80
Santa Rosa, Ca.

My Dad keeps a record collection in cardboard boxes lined up along his bedroom wall collecting New Mexican dust. His prize is an original Al Jolson 78 with the jacket taped and even the tape is ripped. Last time I saw him he tried to bribe me into taking it back to LA and selling it for a bundle. He's convinced it's worth at least a grand. Maybe more, depending on the market. He says he's lost touch with the market these days.

My Dad has a picture of a Spanish señorita covered in whip cream pinned above the sink on his kitchen wall. My Dad actually does. He walked me over to it and we both stared at it for a while. "She's supposed to be naked under there, but I'll bet she's wearing something," he said.

He gave me a tour of all his walls. All his walls are covered with pictures. Wall-to-wall magazine clippings. Each picture is a point of view. Like peering out through different windows into intricate landscapes. I stared at the pictures. A waterfall with real rocks glued onto the foreground. Rocks he'd found to fit the picture. A white dog with a green fish in its mouth. Saguaro Cactus in the setting sun ripped from a 1954 *Arizona Highways*. An orange Orangutang fiddling with its privates. A flight of B-52 Bombers in Wing Formation. A collage of faces splattered with bacon grease.

My Dad has a collection of cigarette butts in a Yuban coffee can. I bought him a carton of Old Golds but he wouldn't touch them. He kept twisting tobacco out of butts and rolling re-makes over a grocery bag so as not to lose the slightest bit. He sneered at my carton of cigarettes, all red and white and ready-rolled.

He spent all the food money I'd gave him on Bourbon. Filled the ice box with bottles. Had his hair cut short like a World War II fighter pilot. He gleamed every time he ran his hand across the bristles. Said they used to cut it short like that so their helmets would fit. Showed me how the shrapnel scars still showed on the nape of his neck.

My Dad lives alone on the desert. He says he doesn't fit with people.

4/79
Santa Fe, New Mexico

There's a dead Monarch butterfly on the sidewalk of Ozona. The breeze flops it back and forth. All day they've been exploding into my windshield leaving pink and gold splashes across the glass. I saw one drop vertically from the sky and crash into the blacktop of Highway 10 East. It must be their time of the year to die.

16/10/80
Ozona, Texas

A '59 red Impala, chopped and channeled, with aluminum skirts, slides silently through the lush pastureland of Napa. Only car on the road. It's the first day of the New Decade and I try not to look on this event as a sign of anything. Least of all a sign of time. I'm sitting dead still in a silver truck with my Mother, my Son and my Dog. I can't keep my eyes off the red car. The way it glides. The way it cuts through this deep farming country with a slick city sneer. Its chrome antenna gently slicing air. A wicked wand hunting waves from far off towers.

My Mother's Voice is telling my Son the story of my Grandfather, my Father and the Rooster. It goes like this: "When my Father was just a Little Baby, he was playing on his hands and knees in the chicken yard. His Father (my Grandfather), was watching him from a distance on the porch, sitting in a rocker. A Big Leghorn Rooster went after my Father to peck his eyes. My Grandfather reached down, grabbed a tractor wrench and threw it, tearing the Rooster's head off. My Father never noticed the cause of the action. All he saw was one minute a whole Rooster, the next minute a headless one. My Grandfather went back and sat down in the rocker. My Father kept crawling around on his hands and knees. The Rooster ran in circles in search of its head."

The red Impala disappears behind a hedgerow of Giant Blue Gum Eucalyptus. The Pasture is soaked in rain. I don't feel like moving much. I'd just as soon live in this truck. I'd just as soon let the grass grow right through the tires.

1/1/80
Napa, Ca.

The Muzak has a buzz in it whenever the bass line comes in on the chorus of muted trumpets. (Tijuana Brass.) A Chicano busboy with a neat scar running the length of his nose is hunched under the cash register holding a yellow phone. He looks out of place in his uniform, as though the uniform is unable to socially transform him into being strictly a busboy and a busboy only. He speaks in quick, soft phrases of Spanish. The corners of his eyes curl as though a woman is on the other end.

Short-coupled teen-age guys carrying lock-back knives keep crossing from the counter to the bank of pay phones on the wall.

A man in an orange booth calls out, "Juanita!" to a tall skinny brunette who looks anything but Spanish. She turns toward him, clutching her chest, eyes wide as though not knowing what to expect, recognizes him, rushes toward him saying:

"My God, I heard my name and I thought, 'Somebody knows me!'"

1/79
San Joaquin Valley, Ca.

Three people in this town keep trying to pass their deaths off on to other people. Two women in white nurses' outfits. One man in a blue tuxedo. I know who they are even though I've only seen them from a distance. Always at night. Always huddled in a frantic group at street corners pushing an old wicker chair back and forth between them. Arguing in whispers. Trying to hide their faces. Sneaking around the neighborhood in tennis shoes. I know who they are but I'll never reveal their names.

This wicker chair is the center of their argument. All their terror emanates from this wicker chair. It suddenly appeared one morning in their front yard. They all agreed it was an omen. A sure sign of their imminent death. Now they believe that by leaving the chair in someone else's front yard their death will be averted. But each morning the chair is back in their own front yard.

Tonight they leave the chair in my front yard. I watch them do it. I don't try to stop them. They seem so terrified of getting caught I couldn't stand to catch them. I watch them drop it and run. I hear them running for blocks at top speed, as though afraid the chair might chase them. I watch the chair. It doesn't move. I go down in the cold wind and throw it out into the road but the wind blows it back in my yard. I carry the chair out into the middle of the road and drop it. I run for the house.

I watch the chair from my window. It just sits there in the road. Car lights hit it but it doesn't move. I fall asleep at the window, watching it. In the morning it's back in my yard.

23/7/80
Homestead Valley, Ca.

on a hot day
mayonnaise is supposed to kill you
that's what my aunt told me

she also told me
never to go out without my wallet
in case I got killed
they'd need to identify the corpse

26/4/81
Homestead Valley, Ca.

I've already dropped $82.80 in only two days of playing the Double at Santa Anita. I've fallen into the old habit of shifting my tickets into different pockets, trying to find the lucky one. The right front is usually the hot pocket for the Double. The left front, for straight win tickets and Exactas. The left rear for "Across-the-Board" and "Baseball" wagers. When things get desperate I tend to shift the customary win tickets from the left front and join them with the Double tickets in the right front. The theory is that the heat from the win tickets will cast an influence on the Double or even vice versa. If I win on the front half of the Double then I shift all the Double tickets to the left front pocket, where the win tickets would have been, and back 8/1 or better horses in the second race which I've already included in the Double. All these new win tickets on the back half go into the right front pocket, which is now hot as a pistol having just come off a win in the first race.

Today, none of this is working.

1/79
Santa Anita Race Track
Arcadia, Ca.

they ooze and call each other "darlings"
they hire fortune tellers who lie
they frame pictures of the kids they've sent away
they call the old black bartender by his first name
they hire watered-down R & B bands and make them play
acoustic
they frown on nude swimming
they confess to anyone who'll listen
they each have an "oldest and dearest" friend
he's usually the one they've confessed to the most
they hate being wished "Happy Birthday"

53

they love having not seen someone for such a long time
then they rush to the next one
their loneliness is covered with grins
their loneliness is smothered in a circle of "friends"

25/7/81
Hollywood, Ca.

She kept him up all night, killing mosquito-hawks. She wouldn't
let him sleep. Things kept flying through the open window and
she'd knee him in the ass until he responded.

"Something's flying around in here," she'd say.

"Well, kill it."

"Honey, come on, you know I can't kill bugs. Please? It's a
great big creepy winged thing." Finally, he would throw himself
out of bed, snap the light on and scan the room for the invader.

"Don't kill it, okay?"

"I'm not gonna kill it."

"Just throw it back out the window."

"That's what I'm trying to do. I gotta catch it first."

Capturing the bug live was the part that really pissed him off.
That's what took all the time. It would've been easy just to
squash its silly fuzzy body against the wall. Just cream it in a
corner. But no, he had to hunt the idiot thing down. Follow its
frantic flopping through the bookcase, across his Quarter Horse
magazines, into the closet then back out, up the wall to the bare
light bulb where it went into a whirling frenzy of figure-eights
and tight concentric circles.

54

"It's only a moth. It's not a mosquito-hawk."

"I don't care. I can't stand the way it moves."

"Moths don't bite."

"Please, get him out of here."

"All right."

"Don't kill it though."

"All right, all right."

He teetered on the mattress, reaching for it, making short stabs then long raking sweeps with both arms. She was far below him with the blankets up around her chin and her huge brown eyes peering up as though any second the winged demon would make a dive for her throat. He lashed out suddenly with a devastating right cross that amputated the light bulb clean from the socket. Everything went black. (Sound of showering glass.) He threw himself down on top of her and ripped the blanket away. (She was more worried about the broken glass than the moth by now.) The electronically timed security floodlight on top of the bank across the street went on, filling the room with blue light. He rolled her over. She giggled, then moaned softly as he slowly inched his way inside her.

"You know, what we need is screens," he said as he kept sliding deeper.

"Screens?"

"Yeah, to keep the bugs out."

"Then we couldn't open the windows wide enough. In this heat we need them wide open."

"Yeah, I guess."

"I haven't got my thing in you know."

"Great."

1/7/81
Homestead Valley, Ca.

his canaries
were dropping off like flies
every morning
there'd be another one
stiff
on the floor of the cage

the Vet told him
it was due to bacteria
in their drinking water
but he himself knew
it was down
to the way he was living

2/8/81
Homestead Valley, Ca.

I found a dead water-bird in the middle of a parking lot. There were no cars. The bird was in perfect condition. Still limp and not a sign of blood. I brought the bird home and stuck it in the ice box. The next day me and my Dad took it around the neighborhood asking people if they'd ever seen a bird like that before. Nobody had. We took it to a Taxidermist and he couldn't tell what kind of bird it was either, although we all agreed it must be a water-bird because it had webbed feet. The Taxidermist had this theory that the bird was flying over the parking lot and mistook the reflection off the pavement for a lake. He figured the bird just crashed into the blacktop and broke its neck. This struck me as being such a wild assumption on the part of the Taxidermist that I couldn't stop thinking about it for days. I kept putting myself in the bird's place, flying high above the parking lot, cruising for a lake. Why would a bird like that be so far from where lakes were to begin with? How could a bird get lost?

30/1/80
Homestead Valley, Ca.

I'm surprised at my own nostalgia for times I barely remember living. I never think of myself as going through the Forties. The Forties are reserved for my parents' generation and pilots with fur-collared leather jackets, smiling in front of prop planes.

Small moments open for me sometimes in crossing the kitchen when the sun hits a particular color in the paint job. I go into a reverie from pastel blue of a time of Dairy Cows, very few people, all who knew each other, in a small isolated American Village. Old women who rarely leave home. Old women I go on errands for. A Parrot even older than the women. A horse named "Nigger". A grey Chrysler with plaid seat covers. Sycamore leaves as broad as my chest. A peeling decal on the foot of my bed of an "Adohr" Milk Boy dressed in all white, black-visored cap, rosy red cheeks, carrying a wire basket full of bottled milk. A smell of women. All old. The smell of old women on everything. In the furniture. In the closet. In the drawers, mixed with wood. The sight of my dead Aunt, sitting upright, a lamp lit on her shoulder, one hand limp in her lap. Her knees always confused me. Even in death her knees seemed young and it seemed "wrong" that they should seem that way. I was attracted to her knees. Point blank. The way they went white at the bone-part when she crossed them and the grey silk stockings put pressure on the caps. I was turned off by her feet though. The small rolls of flesh that erupted out of the tops of her shoes. She told me it was due to swelling in wet weather but I could see she was forcing her feet into some vain idea of smallness. Petite Betty Boop mythology. It was this contradiction between her feet and her knees that led me to see broader contradictions in myself. Later, I secretly thanked her feet for this.

I waded out into the rain. I got far away from people under the spell of Pepper trees and purple Crayfish. I fished red-striped golf balls out of mud holes made from their own impact. I remember the thrill of finding one had to do with the fact of it being lost by somebody else. Had to do with the fact of it being lost out of failure. That some stranger had smacked it clear out

57

into the wilderness and human eyes had never seen it since. Raccoons had walked across it, Jays had poked at it, Squirrels had tried to lift it, but here, me, the first human, pops it out with a thumb, washes it clean in the stream and sells it back to some fool at the Clubhouse for a buck. Sometimes the same fool who lost it to begin with. I could always tell the squirming guilt of recognition in their eyes.

These were days when I must have been small because every face seems bigger than life size.

21/12/79
Homestead Valley, Ca.

There was a black-out in Oaxaca the night they drove in. Candles lit the lobbies of every hotel. There were no rooms.

They finally found a place called the Hotel Nacionale on the north side of town. The doors of each room were composed of vertical metal bars, just like small-town jail cells he'd seen in Montana. The occupants of each room were openly visible to them as they climbed the stairs with their luggage. The tenants appeared to be mostly derelicts and alcoholics – sprawled on the floor, hanging halfway off stained mattresses, propped up in corners, staring deeply at the concrete floor.

They quickly locked the door behind them, hid their bags under the bed and searched frantically for the toilet. There was no toilet. Only a sink in the corner. They took turns climbing the sink and letting "Montezuma's Revenge" rush out of them. They found themselves laughing at the situation but felt they should suppress it since the others, suffering in their cells, might think they were laughing at them.

They kept up this exchange all night long with no relief in sight, one of them resting on the mattress while the other one straddled the sink. Sometimes one of them would vomit while the other one tried to hold back. Sometimes they would vomit together and that made them laugh even harder, to the point where they were afraid they might choke on their own puke.

They kept the blue candle burning all night in the window. Firecrackers exploded from the street below. They could hear kids running. Quetzal birds screaming from palm trees. The tenants moaned and shouted out in Spanish to no one in particular.

They stopped laughing after a while and just lay on the mattress together, staring up at the patched plaster. Wet patches where the plumbing was seeping. They both had the chills. They didn't speak. He was thinking about a pool hall named Julian's on 14th Street. She was afraid she might die.

6/9/80
San Rafael, Ca.

down on both knees
elbows poking into the night

it's true
this deep connection
it's really true

the earth gives off a message
it breathes out
I catch it on the inhale

skunks
dead rabbits
the day's heat escapes

you're on a train somewhere
I can see you staring out the window
somewhere outside Salt Lake City

I'm right here
hanging out the window

29/4/81
Homestead Valley, Ca.

I was banking on finding Bill in the apartment I last remembered him in. I tried to visualize it before I got there. The front of it. Right next to the Police Warehouse on Sixth Avenue. He answered the door in his usual state of relaxed fatalism. He was never surprised to see me no matter how long it had been.

His apartment was always cold because of the high ceilings. The TV was on in the bedroom. On the floor, in a circle around the bed, were plates of spoiled food. Mostly Blue Cheese and Ravioli or some other frozen-type Italian dish. Three bottles of Harvey's Bristol Cream stood around the phone on a small night table. Bill crawled back on top of the bed, where he'd been when I rang the buzzer. His body looked like a little boy's with the head of a middle-aged man. He always struck me as physically strange but I never mentioned it to him.

He continued eating a bowl of dry salad and watching *The Johnny Carson Show*. He was sitting on a copy of *Esquire* and the Sunday *Times* was strewn across the bed like he'd raped it. I was glad he was just continuing with his life and not trying to make a show of interest in me. Not asking me what I'd been doing or how I'd been doing or any of that stuff. He just continued with the salad, an occasional slug of Bristol Cream and stared at Johnny Carson.

"What you been doin', Billy?"

"Me? I abandoned my film."

"The one with Charlie?"

"Yeah."

"The one where Charlie rips the head off the dove?"

"Yeah, that one."

"What happened?"

"I lost the continuity."

He set the salad bowl down on the floor on top of a plate of old steak then reached for a pack of Blue Trues. He didn't go on talking until he'd lit one and made a sharp spitting sound on the exhale. (This was a left-over mannerism from when he used to smoke Camels.)

"I couldn't get excited about continuing. That was it. That was mainly it. Plus, the snake died in the middle of it."

"Snake?"

"Yeah, the Boa Constrictor we had. You remember the Boa?"

"Oh, yeah."

"Well, it died. We went up to Massachusetts to put some of the film together and left the snake here in the house. Forgot about him completely. He curled up in the fireplace and died. Landlord smelled it down the hallway and thought I'd died. I mean it must've really stunk up the place. Landlord called the Cops and the Cops thought I was dead. They broke the door down but all they found was the snake."

"So you couldn't shoot without the snake?"

"Theoretically, yes. But the thrill was gone."

That night I slept alone on his couch. The windows were big in front of me. The trees were dark and the wind on that part of Sixth Avenue sounded like it was blowing down through a canyon. Moaning. Coming from way up in Central Park and moving steadily down, gathering its voice as it came. I remembered the Santana Winds in the Valley. The "Devil Winds". The high heat of the night. The fantasy of having a girl. A particular spectacular Chicano girl with slits up both sides of her grey skirt.

Tiny silver crosses flashing below her ears. A King Snake I shot through the neck. Quail scratching around in the orchard. Twin Indian girls across the street and how they used to undress in front of their window. Silver Dollar Eucalyptus. Fields of Bird of Paradise. I heard gun shots on Sixth Avenue. Gun shots or backfires. Or backfires that sounded like gun shots. I tried to think of what it was I was supposed to do but felt it was already done. Whatever it was. I heard two voices laughing hysterically on the street. Two black female voices and nothing else. They were laughing so deeply and so beyond themselves that I knew they were out of danger. I remembered how once I'd mistaken a laugh like that for a scream. On Avenue C. How I'd rushed down to the street half naked. A girl was pinned to a plate glass window by a tall man in a suit. She told me to "Fuck off!" I remembered how King Curtis got killed like that on 23rd Street. I knew I'd often mistaken sounds for other sounds. Like someone breathing right beside me in bed, sounding like a distant fire. I knew now to watch myself.

Bill had fallen asleep with the TV on. A Late Movie. The voice of Ray Milland in *Man with the X-Ray Eyes*. The part where he's screaming at the end. I knew because I'd seen it before. I could see his milky-white eyes on the ceiling. I could smell the Blue Cheese and Bristol Cream drifting in through the open door. Ray Milland's voice seemed to carry the smell. I remembered that Bill's father had died too. Just like his snake. He told me he'd stayed with his father's body for three days afterward. Just sitting in the same room, staring at the corpse. Finally he'd reported the death and found out his father had left him some money. He lost most of it at Aqueduct. The rest he sank into his film.

The Garbage trucks were already grinding away on the street. I hadn't slept and I wasn't about to lie there all night waiting for sleep to catch me. I walked the whole distance to the Lower East Side. The sky was a light pale turquoise. Transvestites stumbled out of the White Tower, sucking glazed donut sugar off their thumbs. One of them asked me if I wanted a blow-job. Cheap.

I climbed the stairs to the Second Avenue apartment. The same journey I'd made habitually for two years straight suddenly felt like a test. Pushing in on the Police Lock, all the other times of pushing in on the Police Lock went through me. As though the body remembered. My chest felt tight and my mouth was dry, like I'd been doing Speed but I hadn't. The rooms felt abandoned but I knew she was in there without seeing her. I could feel her mourning somewhere. I knew she could hear me.

She was sitting on the bed with all the curtains drawn, her legs crossed under her and her head hung down between her knees. Red hair hiding her face. I knew she wouldn't attack me. I wasn't afraid of her physically. I touched her head. It was stiff. As though she'd been in that position for hours or days. The lap of her skirt was wet. Her nose and eyes were running but she wasn't sobbing. Her eyes were deeply inside like she'd seen the last she wanted to see of Real Life. I tried to hold her but it was ridiculous. She was locked in position. I asked her if she wanted something. Like tea. Like Hot Chocolate. Like things I used to ask her late at night when we first started living together. Each offering seemed more pathetic and further away from her need. I rubbed her neck. It felt like wood. She made a sound. I asked her something else but she was incapable of words. Nothing came out of her but a kind of stuttering consonant noise. Then she went silent again. I found a piece of paper and a pencil and set them in her lap. Again, the sound came out of her in little spits: "Dtha, dtha, dthaa, dtha, dtha." I put the pencil between her fingers and moved her hand around on the paper showing how the lead was capable of making marks. She stared at the lines. No sound. I let go of her hand and she continued moving the pencil, first in weak circles then smaller dark circles. The sound came back to her as she scribbled: "Duth, duth, du, du, duth...." I watched her fingers remember the gestures of drawing. First an aimless uncoordinated scrawl. Then, slowly, firmer strokes with intention behind them. Lines connecting with lines forming a small body with wings and a tail, then feet. Little webbed feet, then a head with a beak. The bill of a duck. "Du, du, du, duck." She pronounced it, jerking her head at me with a sudden kid's smile then hiding again in her hair. "Duck!" I took the pencil from her and wrote "DUCK" underneath the drawing. I repeated the word to her. She fell straight back on the bed clutching her legs and clawing at her stomach. I tried to hold her head as she thrashed back and forth. She moaned in a voice I'd only heard in animals giving birth. Mares moaning. Sheep. It kept rolling out of her as her body unleashed itself. At the peak of it I thought for sure she was dying.

It suddenly left her. She was instantly transformed. She started using words as though she'd never known the lack of them. She stood up, moved toward a change of clothes, brushed her hair, wiped her cheek bones with fast flicks of her fingers, picked up the phone, dialed across the Hudson, sat on the bed and smiled at me without the slightest recognition of where she'd just been.

"Hi, Mom? It's me. Listen, are you feeling okay? That's good Mom. Look, I thought I'd come up there and see you. Would you like that? Just a little visit. Would you like me to come up?" She paused and smiled at me then stared at her little fingernail. "Yes, I can leave right away. No, he's gone. I don't know where he went. He doesn't live with me now. No. I don't know. He's taken off somewhere. I'll see you soon, all right? I love you too, Mom."

10/78
Homestead Valley, Ca.

If you were still around
I'd hold you
Shake you by the knees
Blow hot air in both ears

You, who could write like a Panther Cat
Whatever got into your veins
What kind of green blood
Swam you to your doom

If you were still around
I'd tear into your fear
Leave it hanging off you
In long streamers
Shreds of dread

I'd turn you
Facing the wind
Bend your spine on my knee
Chew the back of your head
Til you opened your mouth to this life

31/1/80
Homestead Valley, Ca.

I used to bring Nina Simone ice. She was always nice to me. She used to call me "Daahling." I used to bring her a whole big gray plastic bus tray full of ice to cool her Scotch.

She'd peel off her blonde wig and throw it on the floor. Underneath, her real hair was short like a sheared black lamb. She'd peel off her eyelashes and paste them to the mirror. Her eyelids were thick and painted blue. They always reminded me of one of those Egyptian Queens like I'd seen in *National Geographic*. Her skin was shining wet. She'd wrap a blue towel round her neck then lean forward resting both elbows on her knees. The sweat rolled off her face and splashed on the red concrete floor between her feet.

She used to finish her set with the "Jenny the Pirate" song from Bertolt Brecht. She always sang that song with a deep penetrating vengeance as though she'd written the words herself. Her performance was aimed directly at the throat of a white audience. Then she'd aim for the heart. Then she'd aim for the head. She was a deadly shot in those days.

The one song she sang that really killed me was, "You'd Be So Nice to Come Home To". It always froze me in my tracks. I'd be out on the floor collecting Whiskey Sour glasses and she'd start that rumbling landslide piano with her ghostly voice snaking through the accumulating chords. My eyes would go up to the bandstand and stay there while my hands kept on working.

I knocked over a candle once while she was singing that song. The hot wax spilled all over a businessman's suit. I was called into the manager's office. The businessman was standing there with this long splash of hardened wax down his pants. It looked like he'd come all over himself. I was fired that night.

On the street outside I could still hear her voice coming right through the concrete walls: "You'd be Paradise to come home to."

28/9/80
San Francisco, Ca.

Men combing their hair in cars
Men watching their hair in rear-view mirrors
Men carrying big black combs in their back pockets
Men worried how Women will see them
Men turning themselves into advertisements of Men

Women wearing boots that make them limp
Women watching their eyes don't wander on to the eyes of Men
Women worried how Men will see them
Women turning themselves into advertisements of Women

This little girl wearing a pale green dress and black, high-topped sneakers.

This little girl chasing a tiny piece of cellophane blowing across a vacant lot.

This little girl speaking to the cellophane as though it was a being of the wind.

This little girl giggles at the hot tropical breath on her back. She feels no separation between herself and the cellophane. Both being blown. Both being together in the same moment. She stares it down. She speaks directly to this cellophane:

"Just let me step on you," she says. "Just stay still so I can step on you," she says.

13/1/80
Homestead Valley, Ca.

It's a high crime night. The cops are out in hot pursuit. The moon is frozen full. Sleepers are having bullet dreams. Sirens weave through a thousand streets.

In one kitchen far away a woman has gotten herself into deep water with a man. She's scared but it's coming out angry. He's drunk and it's turning mean. He's already blown a hole the size of a wrecking ball through the front door. Ragged wallpaper flutters. The night leaps in at them. No scream is heard because there's no one to hear it. No phone. No car because he's got the keys. She sees him shaking with rage. His own. A rage of unknown origin. She sees him fumbling with the plastic green shotgun shells. She makes a dash for the hole in the door. He falls on his face. She's loose in the cattle yard. No shoes. Sinks to the knees in muddy manure. Hears a shot from the porch. Waits to feel it. Nothing. Pulls her legs out with both hands. Heads for the light on the hill. Can't remember who the light belongs to. Can't remember if the light belongs to people or just some barn. A light is better than no light, she thinks. Any light is better than dark. She's falling in deep plow ruts. Clawing her way. Any light is better than dark.

18/1/80
Petaluma, Ca.

horrible idiot cartoon voices
animal idiot cartoon voices
while the sea wind wails
and these sightseeing ferries
come leering by

lots of dead fish
floating
lots of dead fish

now a pretend scream
real sirens
some short shots

stink of Gold Tequila
through the morning skin

30/10/81
Seattle, Wa.

Certain thoughts I'm afraid might actually come true. I mean, not the thought so much as the thing the thought's about. The subject of the thought. Like, for instance, I might think that I accidentally cut my head off with a chain saw. I see it. In the thought. The thought provokes this picture: (Head flying. Neck bleeding. There I am. Standing in a field. Underneath an oak tree. My red chain saw is above me. Meadowlarks are singing. A Redwing Blackbird lands in the tree. The chain saw kicks back and chops my head off.) I shake my head saying to myself, "No! Don't think thoughts like that! They might come true." Sometimes the thought leaves when I say that. But a lot of the time it comes back. And a lot of the time it comes back as a version of the original thought. Like, for instance, this time it will come back like this: (There I am. Standing in a field. Underneath an oak tree. My red chain saw held above me. A Meadowlark is singing in the distance. A Hawk soars in circles. A Dog barks. The Chain Saw kicks back and cuts my arm off.)

If I happen to be working with a chain saw at the same time this type of thought comes up I immediately get superstitious about elements of the thought which connect with the action of the Chain Saw amputating different parts of my body. For instance, if in actuality a Redwing Blackbird lands in the tree I'm working on or a Hawk soars or a Dog barks or a Meadowlark sings I immediately start taking these events as omens. I stop the chain saw. Sit down quietly under the Oak Tree and just relax. Now, I begin to be afraid, not of the consequences of the thought so much as the thought itself. I start hoping the thought doesn't · come back. I start straining against it. Trying not to let it in. Then I start to get a little courage up and I go the opposite direction. I start to dare the thought. I invite it in: (There I am, sitting under the Oak Tree, inviting a dangerous thought. Meadowlarks are singing. A Cow moos. A Redwing Blackbird lands on a fence post. The thought bursts in. Motor roaring. Blood and guts. My head flies off. I'm getting tense. Then I just watch it. Like a movie. Now it starts to behave in a different way. It starts to behave itself. It stands still. The life goes out of it. The picture dissolves. The thought disappears. I'm left in one piece. There I am. Sitting. Without a thought in my head. Meadowlarks are singing. A Redwing Blackbird lands on a fence post. Dog barks. Cow moos. Peacock screams. Bus goes by. Cat meows. Chain saw growls in the distance.)

31/3/81
Santa Rosa, Ca.

I keep praying
for a double bill
of
Bad Day at Black Rock
and
Vera Cruz

28/4/81
Santa Rosa, Ca.

They lost the Navajo radio station about sixty miles east of Gallup on Highway 40. It just faded into thin air. The ancient drums began to mix with McDonald's commercials and Tammy Wynette then finally got swallowed whole by White American News: "England vs. Argentina". They'd driven thirty-two hours, straight through the night from way up above Modesto. Swapped driving for sleeping between them but sleep wouldn't come to either one of them so they ended up sitting side by side singing old Hank Williams songs and watching the sun come up on the highway. The women had no trouble sleeping. They lay curled up in the back in various terminal attitudes. Dead to the world. They could sleep through anything. It was amazing.

A certain crazy state of mind started to take hold of the two men. They passed through the territory of inner complaining about not having enough sleep and went straight into a kind of ecstatic trance. Their bodies gave up the ghost and they began to tell stories, mixing the past and present at random.

"I remember I was on a plane and I had a crewcut and a grey suit and tie. This was 1957 and I was on my way to College in Arizona. This was going to be my first time ever in the West. Arizona State College – 'The Sun Devils'. So uh – I remember having this big idea of formality connected with College because my whole orientation had to do with Ivy League schools since I was from Jersey City and I'd always lived on the East Coast. So I tried to imitate that way of dressing, thinking everyone dressed like that no matter where they went to College. Anyway, the plane lands in the desert and I step outside and I've never been in the West before and I'm thinking, 'this is great, this is my first time out West and here I am stepping out into it,' and all of a sudden this gigantic blast of hot air hits me in the face. It's like a furnace. I figure I've walked right into the props of the plane or something. I mean I've never felt such intense heat before. Just the heat of the desert. And I'm sort of staggering down the ramp of the plane trying to catch my breath and the second thing that hits me is this overpowering smell of cow shit. Cow shit every-where. And then the third thing is this guy, a sort of delegate from the College that they'd sent out to meet me. He was a senior or something. A Wrestling Champion. He had his Wrestling Champion jacket on. A very short, stocky kind of blonde guy with a flat top, jeans turned up at the cuffs and a polka-dot shirt. I thought, 'This guy is dressed just like we dressed ten years ago back East.' So those were my first three strongest impressions of the West. It's hotter than Hell. It smells like shit. And every-body's behind the times."

They missed the Santa Fe turn-off by a good twenty-five miles. Just sailed right past it. It wasn't until they were almost into Pecos that they realized their mistake. They'd already made a pact back in California not to stop the truck unless it was absolutely necessary. So they switched drivers in mid-stream. Let the truck crank down to about 35 mph while the one behind the wheel slid out from under it as the other one squeezed down into the seat. It was a good method. They lost no time retracing their route. As the truck swung a wide U-turn off Highway 85, one of the women spoke up. She'd been sleeping on the floor on her back and she sat straight up. She staggered toward the front and reported this dream to the driver:

"We were all in Arizona but it felt like I was alone. And I was in this little Indian pueblo and I kept on getting glimpses of secret little magic rituals down the alleys. Right at the very ends of these alleyways. Indians appearing and disappearing. One of the things I saw was this brilliant red terra-cotta kind of dust being thrown on the slope of a little mesa. I couldn't see who was throwing it though. And then someone would throw this blue Lapis Lazuli dust on the red dust and the two would mix in some special way. Then this guide guy came along. He was like a very reserved, very thin English Graham Greene kind of character, in a loose white suit. His suit would ruffle up from the wind. I followed him into the mesa and he took me into this place that was like an abandoned meat packing plant with a lot of different levels – all made out of concrete and painted dark green and white. There were these metal grids and catwalks we crossed. I followed him into this one room that was a lot like being outside. Then this guy started to take off his jacket. He had these huge muscles and his whole body was covered with freckles. Then his face changed into a very smooth, bland expression, also covered with freckles. He gave me the impression he was now going to reveal something very important. He twisted his torso to the side and lifted his arms as though he was about to start a race. It looked like he was going to go through a whole series of poses but all he did was flex his muscles in a rhythmic kind of repetition. Sort of pulsing all over from the waist up."

In Santa Fe they only stopped long enough to gas up and then headed north toward Chimayo. The sweet smell of Juniper blew through the open windows. Crows floated above the highway scanning for dead lizards and rabbits. The Black Mesa appeared on their left and they all agreed that they understood why the Indians considered it sacred. But none of them actually explained why they thought that.

They pulled up in front of the Santuario de Petrero – a small adobe church nestled in a grove of leafless Cottonwoods. Black-haired kids were playing baseball in the red sand next to the church but none of them looked up at the new arrivals. An old German Shepherd lay on his side in the dirt. Beside him was a dead Muscovy duck with its head ripped off. It looked like the dog had been playing with the dead duck for hours and had slowly grown tired of it. The dog blinked at them as they passed but didn't get up. Didn't even raise his head.

The main church was closed. A big padlock hung on the oak doors. They circled the outside of the church looking for a way in, but every entrance was locked. They crossed the plaza and found a smaller chapel with the door wide open. Inside there were rows of old wooden benches with an aisle of turquoise-blue linoleum running up the middle. The linoleum was tacked down along the edges with aluminum stripping. The altar was crowded with all kinds of Catholic saints and figures dressed up in Elizabethan-type clothing. Seven-foot plaster statues of the Virgin Mary with her arms outstretched. Plastic flowers in tall Mexican pots. Little tin tuna cans for burning incense. Prayer candles. Good-luck candles. Money candles. Health candles. In the very center of the altar was a glass case with brass trim containing a child's doll dressed in white lace with a red ribbon around its head. The doll's eyes were wide open. Directly above the case a six-foot wooden crucifix hung on the wall. The face was in total anguish and the eyes were looking straight down at the doll. To the right of the altar was a blue flower-print curtain covering a narrow doorway. One of them went up to the curtain and parted it. Behind it was a three-foot square pit in the bare ground filled with red clay dust.

The woman who had told the dream about Arizona got suddenly spooked and ran out of the chapel into the courtyard. She kept running straight toward the truck. A white dog ran right up to her, barking ferociously as though she was trespassing. She stopped. The dog stopped. They stood there staring at each other for a while then slowly the dog turned and walked away without looking back at the woman. It was just now beginning to get dark and the only sound was the distant rumble of a Low-Rider's Chevy.

The next day they drove out past the race track to visit the father of one of the men. He was sitting hunched over in a Maple rocker with stained pillows strapped to the seat and back. He was just sitting there in a barren cement room. His beard was long and red. His hair stood up at the back like a rooster. He wore an old black quilted jacket that had faded yellow spots from the sun. His hands trembled as he made a vain attempt to stand for the visitors but couldn't make it more than halfway before he dropped back into the rocker breathing in short desperate bursts. His eyes were blue and wild with a frightened child-like amazement. He hadn't been visited in quite a while. On the floor beside him was a bottle of Dickel's Sour Mash in a brown bag, a white plastic plate overflowing with cigarette butts and a small cardboard box with newspaper sticking out the top of it. A short Mexican man stood beside the father, sort of leaning toward him as though he might have to protect him from the intruders. He had grey eyes that were cast over like an ageing horse about to go blind. He introduced himself as Steve Sandoval and he explained that he'd taken the old man out for a car trip yesterday to get some fresh air. On the trip he said he had predicted to the old man that he would have visitors soon. Probably his family. He said he just had a feeling.

74

The father reached down and picked up the small cardboard box. He began pulling objects out of it wrapped in newspaper. His hands shook violently as he peeled away the newspaper and revealed a black and white plastic horse with a rubber saddle. He handed it to his son. The father kept unwrapping more objects. A silver belt buckle with a star and the words State of Texas running around the star in a circle, a small green ceramic frog with somebody's initials carved into the bottom, a black rock from the High Desert. The son kept collecting all the objects in his lap and wished he'd brought something for the old man. He took off his straw Resistol cowboy hat, reached over and placed it on his father's head. It fit perfect.

They tried to get the old man out of the room into the sunshine so they could take some pictures of the whole family together. He stumbled just outside the door and fell into a curtain of aluminum flip-tops from empty beer cans that he'd strung together himself. He cursed the gravel under his feet and staggered toward a little patch of brown grass. He stood in the middle of the grass and proclaimed that he'd planted it himself. "The only real lawn in town," he said.

They helped him back inside where he collapsed into his rocker again. They said goodbye to him there and he clasped all their hands very firmly. They were surprised he had that much strength left.

It took them a day and a half to reach Needles. They told each other they wanted to relax this time on the return trip. That it wasn't necessary to drive like demons through the night. When they stopped for gas they got an old guy inside the Shell Station to take a picture of all of them together, standing in front of the truck. The old guy's hands shook as he tried to figure out how to focus the long zoom lens.

They hit the Mojave with a full tank and not a doubt in their minds that they'd reach Barstow. The driver remembered reading somewhere that this was the exact route that Merle Haggard took back in 1957 when he was fleeing Flagstaff and the

Highway Patrol. Except Merle had done it on foot in November in the freezing cold, hitching rides with drunk Apaches and jumping trains, only to get busted again in Bakersfield. The driver also remembered another time when he himself had been here on this desert as a teenage kid.

"It was right near Barstow somewhere. Some little town I don't even remember the name of. Probably just the outskirts of Barstow is all it was. We'd driven out from Cucamunga where my friend lived. Ed Cartwright. He was crazy. Always on Benzedrine. Used to bring lunch sacks full of Mexican Bennies to High School. Trade kids their dessert for a Bean. Hostess Twinkies and stuff like that. We were both on the Track team. Me and Ed. Both ran the 220. In fact we both broke the League record in the same year. They couldn't believe it. Two guys from the same school broke the League record, which had stood for about fifteen years I think. I think it was around twenty-three seconds. Something like that. We'd fly on those Beans. Nobody knew we were cranked up of course. All they knew is that on certain days we'd run sort of average and then on other days we'd turn into these manic rocket machines. You'd feel like you were having a heart attack in your Adam's apple after a sprint like that. Took you about a week to recover because you'd rip all your thigh muscles up, not being able to feel the pain during the race. I mean there was no pain. Just this overwhelming sense of speed and victory. Anyway, Ed picks me up one morning in his '58 Impala. That was the first hot year for the Impala. 350 engine I think. Which was big for those days. Had that really beautiful rear end with the chrome curling down around those three red tail lights on each side. I sorta preferred the fins on the '57 Bel Air myself but this new Impala was a real smoker over a quarter mile. Used to blow off everything in its class at Irwindale Drag Strip. So anyway, Ed picks me up real early. He was always an early riser. In fact I don't think he'd hardly sleep at all when he was chunking Beans. We took off out through the grape vineyards on the old Baseline Highway. That was his favorite stretch because the Highway

Patrol rarely cruised it. They preferred the action down on Foothill or the Pomona Freeway. That's where they'd really hook you. Ed loved Baseline and he never took his foot off the floor once until we reached Cajon Pass.

"Once we got up over the mountain he told me he had an Uncle who was a desert rat. Lived out in a tin shack somewhere. Played the piano and raised goats. Real loner. He said the guy was great though. Give us all the whiskey we wanted. I told him I'd never drunk whiskey. All I'd ever drunk was Ripple Wine and Country Club Stout Malt Liquor. Usually in tandem. Ed said I'd never really drunk, then. It turned out he was right.

"When we finally got to the shack it was about one in the afternoon and the heat was unbelievable. I mean, Barstow cooks in the summer. Must've been a hundred-and-twenty or something. You could see these purple bluish-green heat waves sort of shimmering off the tin roof. Goats everywhere. All kinds of goats. Standing on the porch. Tied to tractor tires. I couldn't figure out what they were eating. Looked like they were just standing around chewing on sand. There was nothing out there. As we drove up closer you could hear piano music sort of leaking out through the walls of the shack. Really great old-time stride stuff. Sorta like Tatum but not that fancy. More like Little Brother Montgomery, I guess. No frills. So we go inside. Ed knocks and then just walks right in without waiting. So I follow him. And there's this old guy banging away on an old upright with the veneer peeling off it. Never stops playing. Never turns around or anything. Just keeps playing. He had a black electric fan set up on top of the piano blowing straight into his face and he was wearing a straw hat pulled down over his eyes so it wouldn't blow off. There was a bottle of whiskey and a glass on the stool beside him. The whole place was buzzing with flies. Bluebottle Flies. Horse Flies. Just about every kind of fly you could imagine. Flies fucking other flies. They were crawling all over the guy's neck and arms and landing on his hands and walking across his lips and up his nose but he never stopped playing the piano. It

77

was like he was in this trance or something and we just stood there like a couple of idiots until he finally finished the piece he was playing. It was called 'Madagascar'. That's what he told us when he stopped. 'Madagascar'. I'll never forget that name.

Anyway, we spent the whole day out there drinking whiskey with him. He gave us all we could handle which turned out to be not all that much. The combination of the heat, not eating, the speed and then the whiskey on top of it made me just about lose my cookies. But I held it all in somehow. Then all of a sudden Ed's Uncle gets this brilliant idea. 'Let's go shoot Jackrabbits!' he

says. 'You wanna?' And his whole face lit up almost exactly like
Walter Houston's face in *Treasure of Sierra Madre*. In fact he
reminded me a whole lot of Walter Houston. Kind of like a little
leprechaun. He got real excited and ran into his kitchen and
started pulling boxes of .22 long ammo out of the cupboards and
then brought out these three pistols that he kept in a green
canvas bag under his bed. He gave us each a pistol and then
dumped a pile of bullets on the kitchen table. We loaded up and
followed him out the back door. He had this funny bowlegged
walk and carried a big black flashlight in his hip pocket. I was so
wasted I hadn't even noticed it was getting dark. We walked out
through the goats and they all came running up to him making a
lot of noise like he was going to feed them or something. He
laughed and just waved his hand away, telling them he'd feed
them later. They all moved away like they understood him. We
walked for quite a while straight out into the desert. Didn't stop
walking for a long time. Nobody talked. I remember it took a long
time for my eyes to get used to the dark. I kept wondering why
the old guy didn't use the flashlight. When I asked him, he told
me it wasn't dark enough yet. Besides, he could see in the dark,
he said. The flashlight was only for 'freezing' rabbits. Just like
deer. They'd get mesmerized by the light and just sit there. Sure
enough, the first one he hit with the beam came to a screeching
stop, twitching his nose in our direction. We unloaded the pistols
into every conceivable part of his body but he never fell over. Just
jumped and twitched with every shot. We reloaded and repeated
the process. This time my thoughts went far away. Every time I
hit the rabbit, every time a bullet ripped through him, I thought
of this girl. This Mormon girl. It wasn't particularly sexual. The
thoughts were soft. They floated through the silences between
shots. I saw her pink lips. Her arms upstretched. I thought of
trying to reach her although I knew she'd moved away a long
time ago. I remembered her voice. I wondered if she ever
thought of me. And I knew right then that things were very
separate from each other. The most intimate things were very

broken off. I watched my hand on the pistol. The repeated green and orange explosions returning to black. The hand lit up then black then lit again. The hand with no connection to the head. The rabbit finally just fell over."

They pulled into San Rafael about 6 a.m. The dogs ran out to meet them but none of them could seem to manage getting out of the truck. The women were asleep and the men just sat there staring at the blue garage door. The streets were very quiet. A light fog rolled in off the hills and nobody moved until the sun was well up.

14/4/82
Bluewater, New Mexico, thru
18/4/82
Barstow, Ca.

Insomnia is a chain
Insomnia is a loop
Insomnia is a vicious circle

Right now
Inside my skull
Inside the bones

My neck turns
Cartilage moves
I like the sound of my own bones

In the midst of this emergency
I think of you
And only you

In the midst of all this sleepless blood
Your pink lips
Your arms upstretched

I can't breathe without you
But this circle of ribs
Keeps working on its own

17/5/82
Lancaster, Ca.

Dew on the garbage can lid. Surprised my hand. Some dream or other my head was in.

Tricky weather. First flood. Fake Spring. Now freeze like this. Good deal I didn't put the beans in early. Like I was planning.

Good to get the stink out of the house anyway. Whatever it was was rotting. Smelled like dead Broccoli.

Coons'll probably turn the whole thing over in the night anyway. Good thing we got the dogs.

Weird night. No sirens. Silent street. No wind to speak of. Good night for stealing gas.

No, can't get it up for adventure. Too cold. Skin sticks to steel in weather like this.

I was in my T-shirt today. Wasn't I in my T-shirt? Wasn't that today? In fact I was out of my T-shirt once today.

Weird. Atomic weather. Earthquakes probably. Probably means earthquakes.

Except the dogs are supposed to go crazy. Run in circles. Get sick. Signs like that.

Maybe something's cracked at the Plant. That Core thing. Nuclear fission or something. Fission or fusion. Something like that. Where it cuts loose. One's the opposite of the other. I forget which.

They'd have it on the radio by now. Except I don't have a radio. They'd have it on somebody else's radio. Then somebody else would call me. Except I don't have a phone. I don't know anybody else anyway.

It's just as well. I'd just as soon not know if you wanna know the truth. I'd just as soon take it as it comes. Not get all het up about it. If I dissolve I dissolve. Nothing to it. Just as soon dissolve in peace.

Except they say it doesn't happen all at once. Supposed to be slow. Tortured like. Belabored. Ghastly breathing.

Nice thoughts. I only came out to empty the garbage.

2/80

Homestead Valley, Ca.

Why am I thinking
"This guy is totally crazy"
Sitting in a country café
Dressed in a black velvet three-piece suit
Smelling like a 14th Street Pimp
Horizontally twitching brown eyes
With no pupil to speak of

Why am I thinking
"This guy is a maniac"
When he asks if it's ever snowed in San Francisco
If Herb Alpert plays classical music

Why am I thinking
"This man is nuts"
When he tells me he's a man of many talents
But he doesn't have time to develop any one of them

Why am I thinking
"This guy is bananas"
When he picks up the cream pitcher
And calls it a "Cute Cow"

I know why it is
It's because he's not concealing
His desperate estrangement from people

12/79
San Anselmo, Ca.

I've about seen
all the nose jobs
capped teeth
and silly-cone tits
I can handle

I'm heading back
to my natural woman

23/11/81
Los Angeles, Ca.

84

He stands still by the smashed suitcase peering down into all his one-time belongings. Crushed soap bars saved from motel showers. Flattened cans of string beans. A mangled map of Utah. Hot tar and blacktop ground into the pure white towel he was saving for his first long bath in a month.

Nothing moves from one end of the highway to the other. Not even a twig flutters. Not even the Meadowlark feather stuck to a nail in the fence post.

He pushes the toe of his boot across the burned black rubber skid mark. Follows the crazy swerve of tires with his eyes. Sour smell of rubber. Sweet smell of sand sweltering.

Now a lizard moves. Makes a fragile fish-like wake with its tail. Disappears. Swallowed in a sea of sand.

Should he try to salvage something? Some small token of the whole collection. A pair of socks? The batteries from his flashlight? He should try to bring her something back. Some little something. Some memento so at least she'd think he'd been doing more than nothing. Just drifting all these months.

He pokes around in the debris with a mesquite stick looking for a present. Nothing seems worth saving. Not even the undamaged things. Not even the clothes he's wearing. The Turquoise ring. The wing-tip boots. The Bareback buckle.

He drops them all on the pile of rubble. Squats naked in the baking sand. Sets the whole thing up in flame. Then stands. Turns his back on US Highway 608. Walks straight out into open land.

17/2/80
Santa Rosa, Ca.

Red Wasatch Mountains glowing in the night
Sounds of Little League baseball under giant lights

Cheers echo off the mountain wall
We cross the creek on foot

Cottonwoods rattle softly overhead
We see the game from where we stand

Little boys racing for the ball
The creek is cold as ice

We find a hand-made bridge
Boards some kids have nailed together

On the other side it's sandy
Smooth stones

The Mountain has a hold on this town
You can feel it from the creek

31/7/80
Cedar City, Utah

We killed a Green Mojave Rattlesnake this morning. Chopped its
head off with a hoe. Cut the rattle off. Threw the body over the
side of a hill, still thrashing. Dropped the head down a long red
clay drain pipe buried in the sand. Some of us wanted to eat the
flesh but the others went ahead and threw it away. In fact they
rushed to throw it away. I had the feeling they were superstitious. One girl handled the rattle like it was a still-living thing.
Nudging it along the top of a table with her pink fingernail.
It did seem to have a lot of life left in it, although it didn't move
on its own.

Tonight I walked down there by the hill looking for a place to sleep but the smell of other dead snakes was too overpowering. Evidently they always throw the bodies in the same place and the power of their rotting flesh has accumulated day by day.

I left that place and walked upwind, keeping in a straight line, straining to see the path in front of me, moving very slow, listening for snakes. The moon was bright white and the heat was still strong from the day. You could feel it coming up out of the ground being drawn by the night air. I settled on a place shaped like a half-circle, looking out over a narrow dark canyon. I leaned my back against a big flat stone. The stone had gathered a lot of heat and felt good on my spine. I drew my knees up under my chin and held the calves of my legs with both arms. I don't know why I was holding myself like that. I knew I wouldn't be holding myself like that if there had been other people around. I kept looking out through the black branches of a burned Manzanita into the Valley. The lights of Pomona to the left and the dark wild hills to the right. I kept wishing for a horse but the thought of snakes interrupted my dream.

I must've stayed up there for three or four hours in the same spot. Just staring. Something nailed me there. Then I left and drove down the long thin Mt Baldy highway, through abandoned lemon orchards, past the old stone pump house made from boulders cleared off the land in 1910. Past Azusa, past Duarte. I took a cold shower at the Best Western Motel in Arcadia, right across from the race track. I walked naked around the room, dripping on the orange carpet, wondering whether or not to turn the TV on, peering out through the curtains at the cars parked in front of each room, each one parked in a numbered space corresponding to a room. I opened my Rand McNally Road Map on the bed and stared at the state of Wyoming. I ran my finger down the Big Horn Mountain Range.

The next morning I was gone.

27/7/80
Padua Hills, Ca.

I watch my kid jump in his dreams
Sleeping sideways in a motel bed

Next door, a couple argues
He keeps saying: "Now, Lorraina, don't!"
She keeps saying: "Why?"

Swimmers splash in the pool outside
Night swimming
No voices
Only the splashing of arms

My kid jumps
Shifts his head on the pillow
A dream runs through him
His voice
No words

The Grand Tetons loom outside our window
Snowless
Blue

The Snake River curls around our bed
Hisses into itself

The guy with the cartridge belt yells out his window
"Watch the language please!" to the couple who argues

The couple goes silent
Giggles

The Rodeo ends
You can hear the trucks

The Elk Horn Café fills up with Bull Riders

The Eagle makes a drive at a Trout

Someone drops a quarter in the Ice Machine
The Machine delivers with a thud

The swimmers leave the pool
They're talking now
But I can't make out the words

The Elk move North
(You can almost hear them)

The Grizzly goes wherever he wants
(Yesterday he ate three hikers)

My kid jumps in his dreams

A gun goes off

The couple screams

My kid wakes up

5/8/80
Jackson, Wyoming

Tonight
They're watering the grave yard in Cody, Wyoming
A dry wind blows across the Rodeo Stands
The National Anthem floats out to the prairie
Sung without conviction
Sung for the sake of convention

There's a bull here called "Cottonmouth" who's never been ridden
The announcer drawls the old adage
"Never been a bull that can't be rode
Never been a cowboy who can't be throwed"

Big wind blows in from the Rockies
Across the Absoraka Mountain Range
Night swallows Wyoming whole
Night keeps us under lights

6/8/80
Cody, Wyoming

My horse has his ears pricked this morning. He's never been up
this mountain before. He looks at every Oak tree, every squirrel
that jumps in a hole. He never spooks. Just looks.

We make it through a cattle gate halfway up and I stop him on
flat ground. He's blowing from the climb and little patches of
sweat break out on his withers. A rancher sits in his green pickup
in the valley just below us. He sits there staring at us. We stare
back. We refuse to move. I don't know why I'm taking his staring
as a challenge. He's so far below us I can't even make out his face.
His eyes could just as easily be staring at nothing. We're on his
land, that's for sure, but we have no bad intentions. No gun. I'm
not even smoking.

I turn away from the truck and scan the marsh land below, out past the highway. By this movement I'm hoping to show the rancher I'm simply out on a pleasure ride. He completes this visual dialogue by driving off. I guess we understand each other.

At the top of the mountain we cut through a flat little meadow with dozens of deer tracks. Another cattle fence meets us with a huge galvanized chain around the gate and three locks the size of softballs hanging off it. The fence and gate are made of barbed wire which anyone could cut with a pair of pliers, but this rancher is talking to me again with his chain and three locks.

We ride the fence-line looking for a hole. Grey Squirrels thick as Grasshoppers. I turn back into the meadow and see a spot that draws me to it. Black rocks spotted with moss. A group of Oaks and a baby Bay Tree. I tie my horse to the tree and take the hacka-more off him. He seems happy just to be standing under a Bay Tree. No flies in this spot.

I sit down on one of the rocks facing my horse's tail. He's still standing absolutely still with his ears cocked. His tail just hanging. His feet planted firm. His eyes blink and every thought in my head disappears.

21/9/80
Novato, Ca.

from the high high grass
to the edge of the blacktop playground
I see you studying me

I see you when you don't know I'm looking
and every look I steal
adds a day to my life

lately you've been hard to catch
or else I'm getting older
one of us is losing for sure

6/11/81
Homestead Valley, Ca.

What I saw was this: From a distance. Four of them. Moving like snakes. Dragging their legs toward the black herd. Like their legs were dead. Pulling their brown bellies across stone. I didn't even recognize them as human at first. Least of all Sioux. I thought they might be dark dogs or something. Deep holes in the prairie. Moving. I couldn't stop watching them move. I wasn't afraid. I knew the wagons were getting farther away. I knew I was being left behind. But I wasn't afraid. I watched them leap. All four of them at once. They dragged the big bull down. Ripped open the neck with their knives. Ripped open the belly. The belly fell out on the prairie. The membrane broke. All the insides rolled out, steaming in the grass. My eyes began to sting. I heard them singing. Not really a song. A kind of screaming as they tore out the tongue and ate it between them. The bull still twitching. His back legs slowly stiffening out. The tail switched. Thin columns of dust rose up and I followed the dust with my eyes. The Tetons loomed behind. All blue. And I watched those mountains glow. And I thought about Boston. And I missed my piano. And I couldn't believe my piano was in the same world, living in the same time and I'd never see Boston again.

17/7/80
San Anselmo, Ca.

I was deep into eighty acres of sprouting new pasture and my head wouldn't stop. I could see down through the fresh green blades into tread marks left by the tractor's last pass. Into the deep depressions of steer tracks when the ground was mud and everything had been eaten to a short yellow stubble. Around the time they cut the fire-break. I could hear my body wanting to go and lie down but my head wouldn't listen. I could see where the time of day was telling itself much clearer out here. How everything out here understood intimately that the sun was leaving. How hawks even were giving it up.

I kept thinking someone back at the barn was calling me. I was actually hearing their voice and turning to see. Nobody was there.

I was turning back into the land and wondering how far to go. Exactly the same question I'd had before when swimming out in the ocean. What's the point where it becomes dangerous to go any further? And I recognized that the point of wondering comes when you think you've gone too far.

18/12/79
Petaluma, Ca.

Jack Montgomery put his arm all the way down my horse's throat. I watched him do it. I stood right there and watched the arm disappear up to the elbow. A little river of green alfalfa drool spilled down on my boots. I watched it run. I watched my horse's eyes roll back in his head and stare at me like a frightened demon. I watched the sun go down behind his head.

Petaluma was turning pale orange.

13/1/80
Petaluma, Ca.

My Dad had this habit of picking at a shrapnel scar on the back of his neck every time he heard a plane go over our land. He'd be stooped over in the orchard repairing the irrigation pipes or the tractor and he'd hear a plane then slowly straighten up, peel off his straw Mexican hat, run his hand through his hair, wipe the sweat off on his thigh, hold the hat out in front of his forehead to shade his eyes, squint deep into the sky, fix the plane with one eye and begin picking slowly at the back of his neck. Just stare and pick. The scar was the mark of a World War II mission over Italy. A tiny piece of metal remained embedded just under the surface. What got me was the reflexive nature of this picking gesture. Every time he heard a plane he went for the scar. And he didn't stop picking at it until he'd identified the aircraft to his complete satisfaction. He delighted mostly in prop planes and this was the Fifties so there were quite a few big prop planes still in the air. If a formation of P–51s went over, he would almost climb an Avocado tree with ecstasy. Each identification was marked by a distinct emotional tone in his voice. There were planes that had let him down in the heat of combat and he would spit in their direction. On the other hand, a B–54 got a somber, almost religious tone. Usually just the minimal code number was uttered: "B–54," he would say, then, satisfied, he would drag his eyes back down to earth and return to his work. It seemed odd to me how a man who loved the sky so much could also love the land.

29/8/80
Santa Rosa, Ca.

They leave Winnemucca in a hurry
The Father stuffing a thousand-dollar jackpot in his pockets
The Son begging to hold a Silver Dollar
Just to touch the Eagle
The Father asking the Son to call it heads or tails
as they roar down Highway 80

The Son calling it tails as it comes up tails
slap in the middle of the map of Nevada

10/8/80
Winnemucca, Nevada

He was just about exactly halfway between San Francisco and LA. He parked the truck on the soft bank of Highway 5, crawled under a barbed-wire fence and headed toward the Harris Feedlot. He found an open field behind the pens and sat down cross-legged in the middle of it. The raw smell of cattle filled his chest. The sun was just setting behind the hills of Coalinga and two broad bands of orange clouds stretched out across the Central Valley like giant hawk wings. He wanted to talk to himself but the stillness of space stopped him. He listened to it. Whippoorwills. Calves calling out. The beautiful moan of a Kenworth diesel. He pictured both cities simultaneously, as though they hung on the extended arms of the orange clouds. Suspended. Tiny San Francisco dangling to the north: innocent, rich and a little bit silly. The sprawling, demented snake of LA to the south. Its fanged mouth wide open, eyes blazing, paralyzed in a lunge of pure paranoia. This was the place to be, he thought! Right here. In the middle. Smack in the belly of California where he could eyeball both from a distance. He could live inside the intestines of this valley while he spied on the brain and the genitals. It was a vain scheme. Already things were pulling on him in two directions. Already he was moving when he wanted nothing but stillness. A huge hand grabbed him from behind. A hand without a body. It carried him up, miles above the highway. He didn't fight. He'd lost the fear of falling. The hand went straight through his back and grabbed his heart. It didn't squeeze. It was a grip of pure love. He let his body drop and watched it tumble without hope. His heart stayed high, tucked in the knuckles of a giant fist.

23/11/81
Coalinga, Ca.

97

Tonight I'm pushing everyone away. I did it all day but tonight I'm vicious about it. I'm camped out by my favorite window and no amount of harmonica playing, rattle of dishes, laughter of voices from other rooms deep in this house can draw me out. The fading light is what I really crave. Cars with their headlights just coming on. Owls testing the fields. This mean streak slowly fades as the real black night rolls in.

I always get weird around Indian Summer. I've noticed this before. My whole organism feels tricked. Just as the body starts to fall in love with flying golden Poplar leaves. The smell of burning Madrone. The wild lure of Fall gets cut to the bone by Indian Summer.

I don't want to be walking around peeling my shirt off these days. I want deep layers of Canadian blankets and fire. Red eye of fire. And dogs. And cold cold nights.

22/9/80
Santa Rosa, Ca.

Maybe I should make a fire. Would you like a fire? I'll make a fire.

Maybe I should rip up the Sunday Paper into tiny pieces and try not to get hung up on the ads.

Maybe I should finish digging the hole I was digging in the back yard.

Maybe I should make a cup of tea and take Vitamin C. Would you like a cup of tea?

Maybe I should just take a walk with no destination.

Maybe I should stay in one place and stay put and stop making up reasons to move.

Maybe we could both have a conversation. Would you like to have a conversation?

14/1/80
Homestead Valley, Ca.

The wind's been blowing for three days straight. Our best friends are breaking apart. Lovers are calling our house trying to track each other down. The dust blows right across our land. Every door in the place keeps banging. The refrigerator slams. All the windows rattle. Coffee keeps being made. Typing goes on in the basement. (Somebody's getting something down.) The whole town's in an uproar, but only at night.

These days I wonder about leaving. But I've seen myself when I leave. Already seen myself.

Next door they're building a window. I plunge into books on the Gold Rush. One thing captures me. Only one. How they buried each other in giant trees. Inside a whole tree. Nailed inside.

Today I bought a new pistol and a new set of tires. My sister-in-law gasps on the phone. Makes vomiting sounds on the phone. Giggles hysterically. Ecstatic over somebody's chest. My wife reads Jung for some reason. Out of the blue. She usually reads Michael Moorcock but today she reads Jung. My parents live apart. Separate lives. In a flash I almost feel I have a grip. The kind of grip that turns on its tail. The tapping goes on next door. The window proceeds. The voices of women dart through the house. The civilized sound of a truck. What is it I want to make something out of? A collection of sound. Scrub Jays fighting across the canyon. The big willow blowing. The people moving. Being moved. The one typing downstairs. The one in the hospital. The one on the train.

The women come back on their bikes. Along with the kid. The smallest one. Face reddest from riding. Full of the wild. The one son of mine. In the night I read him *Call of the Wild*. He calls it "Buck" for short.

"Can I hear more Buck tonight?" Already it's night.

8/78
Homestead Valley, Ca.

100

Exactly a year ago to this day the three of us left her alone in the house and rode our bicycles down to the marsh by the freeway. Poplar and Sycamore leaves were blowing down the street just like they're doing today. We parked our bikes by a metal bench and the three of us sat watching a Snowy Egret poke holes in the mud with its beak. A siren wailed in the distance. A neighbor and his son rode by on their bikes. They stopped by the bench and made adjustments to their hand brakes. They'd just bought a used black typewriter from a Flea Market and the son was anxious to get it home and test it out. We exchanged some conversation with the father. Mostly about his gears. How he liked his gears to be "smooth as silk".

On the way back home an ambulance screamed past us going the opposite direction. The air was cold and reminded me of Fall in New England. Especially Maine. A skinny black kid from the neighborhood came toward us as we neared our house. He said that an ambulance had just been there.

When we reached the house it was empty. She was gone. There was no sign that anything out of the ordinary had happened. The couch was pulled slightly away from the wall but other than that, nothing. There was no note. I called the emergency number and asked if an ambulance had come to our address. The operator made a direct hook-up with the ambulance. I could hear the siren in the distance. The muffled amplified voices of the Paramedics. The rushing sound of the freeway like a river. I pictured her on her back. Through her eyes I saw the upside down trees tick past. The intravenous bottle swinging above her head. Faces of strangers. They had no idea what was wrong with her they said. She had passed out in the house. When she came to she'd called the ambulance. That was all they knew. They were on their way to the Emergency Hospital.

In the waiting room a young doctor with a beard and a slightly peeved attitude inquired about her condition. He asked us if she took drugs. We said no. He asked us if she had a history of psychological disturbance. We said no. He asked us if she spoke any other language than English. We said she knew a little French. He said he couldn't find anything wrong with her, that he'd asked her what the problem was and she'd told him she had to take a shit. He said: "When someone tells me they have to take a shit I can't take their situation too seriously." He advised us to take her home and give her a lot of rest.

She was in one of six beds lined up against the wall, each one partitioned off from the others by long pale green curtains. The curtains would be slashed open periodically by nurses and medics then slashed closed. Between the slashes instantaneous snapshots of a bleeding leg, an exposed stomach, a dangling arm would be revealed. Behind her curtains she was throwing up all over herself while a nurse held a small white plastic dish under her chin. An attendant dressed in white brought a bucket and mop. He had a smirk on his face as he cleaned up the floor. We asked one of the medics what he thought was wrong with her and he said there was no way of telling until they took a blood test. We asked him why she was throwing up and he said it was probably an hysterical reaction. The body in a state of panic. He said he was going to call the Welfare Psychologist to have a look at her.

She kept thrashing around on the bed in a sitting position. Rocking from side to side as though she couldn't gain her balance. Her face was milk-white. Her eyes searched our faces for some recognition, some reassurance that her panic would pass. Strange words came out of her, half German-sounding. They rolled out of her in quick staccato phrases then abruptly stopped and reverted to English. She said her head was breaking. She asked for an aspirin but they told us they couldn't give her any medication until the physician okayed. it. We asked them where the physician was. They said he was on his way. She asked us what was happening to her and her voice would rise as though she couldn't believe an answer was unavailable. She asked us if she was dying. We stood there watching.

The Psychologist came with a clipboard. He had long side-burns and a contrived calmness about him. He asked us if she had ever had a nervous breakdown before. We said no. He asked us if she took drugs. We said no. He asked us if she was American. We said no, English. He said, "Oh, she sounds German or something."

The blood test verified the problem as physical. The psychological angle was dropped. They performed a spinal tap on her and blood turned up in the fluids. They suspected a brain hemorrhage but they wanted to put her through the X-ray Scanner just to make sure. We followed her ambulance to another hospital where the scanner was located. It was night now. Magnolia trees bloomed in the dark.

The scanner verified the hemorrhage. An aneurysm deep in the Basilar Artery of the brain. A surgeon was notified. He told us the chances were very slim that she'd live long enough to perform surgery. He said it was like a time bomb. The vein could rupture at the slightest agitation. Right now all that was keeping her alive was a thin blood clot where the aneurysm had occurred. If the clot broke she would die. They gave her a sedative and she fell deeply asleep.

We all returned to the house and had dinner together. We agreed we should all stick together and eat as many meals together as possible. We tried not to get caught up in our imaginations. Even so, it was impossible not to have pictures of her jumping into our heads. Her eyes. Her hair sticking to her lips. The image of her alone. Passing out. Coming to, alone. Phoning the ambulance alone. Alone inside herself with an unknown demon. I felt a strong need for something like prayer but realized I'd never learned how. I felt suddenly connected to all those who pray in moments of crisis. Prayer did not seem ridiculous, just unfathomable. As mysterious as the urgings behind it. To be connected to the forces of chance is what I would have prayed for. To know that chance was on our side.

The next morning we returned to the hospital. The surgeon

and the physician were taking a hard-line approach with us. We could see that they'd consulted each other on the best way to deal with us. They seemed determined not to minimize the risks. They reiterated statistics and came up with an 80 per cent chance of her dying. They told us brain surgery was still a medical frontier and that the Basilar Artery was the worst possible location for an aneurysm. They showed us charts and X-rays of the brain. Her brain. A ghostly white scheme of bones and veins with a burr-like explosion at the bottom. They talked to us in hushed, conspiratorial voices. They said it was important that she didn't overhear our conversation in case she became alarmed. If she became excited she might bleed. They said it would be at least a week before they could operate due to the swelling around the artery. "This isn't the kind of thing you jump into," they said.

We began making phone calls in search of another surgeon. We called New York, Boston, Los Angeles and finally tracked down the man whom everyone seemed the most impressed with. People's voices would rise an octave at the mention of his name. He had performed this very operation sixty times before and had only one death on his record. They spoke of him like that. Like a race horse. Apparently he was the Wyatt Earp of neuro-surgery. The only hitch was that she had to be moved to the City Hospital where he practiced and all the latest facilities were available. We calculated the risks. The risk of moving her versus the risk of leaving her. Every choice was a gamble.

We followed her ambulance across the Golden Gate Bridge. It was like moving nitroglycerin. The slightest bump could start the bleeding. We watched the ambulance weave silently through the traffic. Through the fog. Paying the toll. Up the hills. Across trolley car tracks. It seemed unreal that ordinary life was being lived all around us in the streets. People waiting for buses. People beginning their day, lunch pails in hand, newspapers tucked under their arms. We were contained in a separate world. Cut off. Locked into each other and the one who rode ahead of us.

In the lobby of the City Hospital there were only two elevators. Dozens of patients, doctors, visitors, nurses and us – all crammed in together watching the lighted numbers slowly descend to the ground floor. Shaved heads. The sallow grey look of Chemotherapy surrounded us on all sides. Obligatory bunches of flowers hanging from hands. The City Hospital was a direct manifestation of the city itself. Everything was a shock.

She was sitting up now in the mechanical bed and the first thing she told us was that she didn't want to know what was wrong with her. She made us promise not to tell her. We promised. The drugs allowed her to relax but she still felt the headache she said. She said the drugs couldn't touch the headache. She apologized for the trouble she'd caused us. We told her not to be stupid. She wanted a cigarette and we gave her one. She kept tossing herself around, reaching for things like an ash tray or matches. Tossing her hair away from her eyes. We tried to impress upon her the need for being quiet without giving away the specific part of the anatomy. She kept saying, "Don't tell me!"

Throughout the week one of us was always with her. We brought her soup in plastic containers, magazines, cassette tapes, pencils and paper. We'd read to her until she fell asleep and stay with her until she woke up. Sometimes we'd sneak out of the room, down the long corridor and get a cup of coffee out of the machine. We'd pass brain surgery patients in various stages of recovery. All with their heads shaved, bandaged like Hindus, grey smocks, Hospital slippers, slowly shuffling down the corridor clutching the stainless steel hand rail, staring out through stark animal eyes like they couldn't recognize the world they'd come back to or remember the one they'd left behind. We got to know the names of all the nurses on the floor. We quickly grew to like some and dislike others. We did imitations of them at home. We began to talk ourselves into the belief that she'd make it through.

Three days later we met the head surgeon. The man with the

reputation for miracles. He was short with slick black hair parted precisely on the left side. He was dressed as though he'd just stepped out of surgery. A sterile blue mask dangled from his neck. His face was firm and expressionless. His dark eyes meant business. He gave the impression of a man whose time was accounted for down to the last second. He shook our hands perfunctorily and spoke with a South Texas drawl. The drawl itself filled me with confidence. "Now let me speak. I understand she doesn't wanna know what her illness is. Now that's fine with me. If she doesn't wanna know I'm not gonna tell her. All I'm gonna say to her is that I'll be performing an operation on her head. She can find out later what it was for."

We began blurting out vague questions, stumbling over each other, using half-understood technical jargon.

"Just let me speak. I haven't got much time here. I've performed this operation a number of times before and I can say there's a 90 per cent chance it'll be successful. That's not 100 per cent. I'm not saying I'm a magician. I have to fly down South tomorrow but I'll be back on the morning we have scheduled for her. We could let one of the other surgeons here work on her but she'll have a better chance with me." He turned and left the room. He knew precisely where he was going and what he'd do when he got there.

Now we began to worry about *him*. What did he mean "down South"? LA? Alabama? He was flying away from here just when we'd found him? What if the plane crashed? What if LA had an earthquake? What if she bled before he got back?

The next day they performed a preliminary angiogram test on her which involved injecting a liquid dye through her blood stream to chart the flow of blood to her brain. A kind of road map to the scene of the accident. Again we were informed of the risks. The dye could irritate the blood clot and dislodge it from its tenuous seating. She could hemorrhage, partially hemorrhage or not bleed at all. In any case, the test had to be done. They wheeled her downstairs.

We all sat in the cafeteria and waited. We watched the student doctors coming on to the student nurses. We watched the bored face of the cashier taking money from the people paying for their food. The face said time was a burden. A day was just another day to be endured until the next day. We watched how the people paying for their food would turn away from the cashier, trays in hand. How their eyes would hunt for an empty table. This small moment of lostness between the paying for the food and the hunting for a table. A moment where their role would disappear and they'd just be standing dumbly balancing jello on a plastic tray, unsure of the next move. We watched the white clock on the wall.

That night she started worrying about her hair. She wanted to know if they'd have to shave it all or just a patch. She'd noticed everybody on the floor had had their head shaved. We made Joan of Arc jokes and she laughed. She said she didn't care. By now she suspected the brain was the problem. She asked how long she'd been in the hospital and she was amazed when we told her. She said she remembered passing out now. She'd been doing some kind of diet exercises which she'd always jokingly referred to as "killer exercises", lying on her back on the floor. When she stood up she'd blacked out. That was all she remembered.

The morning of the surgery she wanted a cigarette. The nurses said no but we gave her one anyway. She made deep satisfied groans as she smoked. She asked us what would happen if she came out of the surgery like a vegetable. She wanted to know if lobotomy was still legal. What would prevent them from doing a lobotomy on her if things didn't work out. She asked us to promise to keep her with us no matter what. No matter how she turned out. We promised. She said she knew we would bring her back to the world.

The surgery took six hours. The infinitesimally small rubber disc, acting something like a tourniquet around the ruptured area of the vein, had slipped from its position. It slipped repeatedly. The eyes of the surgeon witnessing his own fingers indirectly through mirrors informed his own brain of the need for invention. Through all his schooling and practice he was thrown back on intuition and did something he'd never done before. He placed two discs in strategic positions further down the wall of the vein. Reciprocally they fulfilled the function of the more orthodox approach although, he told us later, there would probably be a 50 per cent decrease in the flow of blood through that vein. He said he didn't think there would be any bad consequences although we would have to give her phenobarbital for at least a year to counteract the possibility of stroke.

She lay unconscious in the Intensive Care Unit. We all went in to see her. She was totally unconscious. They said it would take a while for her to come around from the anaesthesia. All the windows were open slightly around her bed and the night wind blew the curtains. It was odd seeing the outside being allowed entry to this sterilized interior. A transparent tube ran up her nose and down into her lungs, held in place by white adhesive tape. Water vapor blew across her face and tiny clear droplets collected on the hairs around her lips. She breathed oxygen with a deep rasp, more like a death rattle than a sleeper. Her eyes were closed and swollen. Red and blue. A bandage covered her head. She looked more dead than alive. Terrifying in her transformation. The impulse to run was as strong as the one to stay. They told us to yell her name and try to get a response. To shake her by the shoulders. We couldn't bring ourselves to shake her. We called her name. She moved her head. Her eyes stayed closed. We squeezed her hand. She squeezed back. We told her who we were. Our names. She squeezed back. The nurses moved quickly from one bed to another. From one state of emergency to the next. Working more feverishly over one. Pumping his chest. Shaking him vigorously by the shoulders until the chalk blue color left his face. We asked them how long it might take. How long she might be unconscious. They said it depended on the person. Different people took longer than others. They said they hoped she'd come around by tomorrow morning. We asked them if that was normal. They said anything's normal under these conditions.

She stayed unconscious for a solid week. Flat out. Doctors rubbed their thumbnails across the balls of her feet. Her feet would twitch. We asked if that was normal. They peeled back her eyelids and examined her pupils, listened to her heart, took her pulse, made marks on clipboard charts, tapped her knee bones. Her legs would jump. We asked if that was normal. Nurses turned her continually so she wouldn't develop bed sores. Washed her. Dried her. Cleaned her nails. Sat her up on bed pans. Helped her move her bowels. Changed her intravenous bottle. Changed the location of the needle in her arm when the vein got too swollen. We called her name. We whispered in her ear. She smiled but she didn't wake up. The man died in the bed next to her. The same man whose face had turned blue. Now his feet were blue too. He was replaced by another man. All week, patients came and went. She stayed unconscious.

The day she opened her eyes, one eye looked straight ahead while the other one stared to the side. The doctors said this was normal. The optic nerve had been disturbed and would slowly realign itself. They passed their fingers in front of her face. Her arms were strapped down so she couldn't pull the tube out of her nose. They said it was important to keep her lungs drained to protect her from pneumonia. We asked her if she knew who we were. She smiled at us but didn't speak. We told her everything had gone all right.

They moved her from Intensive Care because she seemed to be doing better and they needed the bed. They moved her into a room with three other patients all waiting for surgery. All with brain tumors. One of them told us she had a grave plot already paid for. She said if she didn't die she was going to move to Richmond with her husband. She kept calling her cyst a "crypt". She said they'd tried to burn the "crypt" out of her with radiology. She told us she hated one of the patients in the bed across from her. How this other patient had thrown wet paper towels at her and told her to "get fucked". In this new room a TV hung from the ceiling. It stayed on all day blaring color cartoons of inane animals maiming each other. Hollywood Game Shows. *Gunsmoke* re-runs. We asked the nurses if they could shut it off but they said it was being paid for by the other patients. A woman across the hall kept screaming for her nurse by name even when that nurse wasn't on duty. She had a favorite nurse. When the nurse came she would stop screaming and just moan. When the nurse left she'd start screaming again.

We began to learn how to time our visits according to the drug schedule she was on. Early in the morning she was at her best. Her energy was highest. She could sit up while we fed her. It was the first real food she'd had since the surgery. We'd put a spoonful in her mouth but she wouldn't chew. The food would just sit there. We'd tell her to chew. She'd wait a long time just staring with the food hanging in her mouth. We'd keep telling her to chew. She'd start chewing methodically as though the jaw was obeying instructions from a distant authority with no connection to the act of eating. When the food was reduced to almost a liquid state she'd keep chewing. We'd tell her to swallow. She'd keep chewing. The food would pour out the sides of her mouth. We'd tell her to swallow. She'd stop chewing and stare. She'd swallow and grimace. We'd start all over with a new spoonful. She seemed to recognize us now and started to speak in a little girl voice. The words would come out in short blurts like codes from a mixed-up machine. Her head would jerk sharply to the side in the direction of noises or the slightest movement from objects, like dust balls blowing across the floor or paper flapping in the trash can. "Zat?" she would say, and we would tell her what it was. Once she would start to question these small distractions we couldn't get her to return to eating. She would stare at the suspended spoonful of food and weep. Her whole body would weep. Then she'd fall asleep and we couldn't wake her up for hours.

The bandage was off her head now and the huge scar was in the shape of a perfect question mark ending just behind the right ear. Her head was shaved close but grey and black stubble was already beginning to appear. The scar marked a borderline between the grey and black hairs. All grey on one side. All black on the other. The stark impression of an Auschwitz survivor was impossible to avoid.

They had her sitting up in locked wheel chairs but she couldn't raise her arms to feed herself. She could stand with the aid of the nurses but would drop back down in the chair exhausted after a few minutes. She would sit and stare at the floor in front of her. Her head limply tilted to one side. She would cry silently, her whole face distorted in a grimace of pure grief as though she was mourning the loss of her own life. A life dimly remembered. She said she couldn't remember how she got there. Her whole body would weep and we'd hold her until she fell asleep.

Physical therapists began working with her, trying to get her to walk. They would do pushing exercises with her. Pulling exercises. Coordination exercises. Touching her fingers together. Lifting her feet an inch off the floor. One therapist had a Boston accent and she thought he was funny. She made a face whenever he came in the room and he pretended he wasn't bothered by it.

A speech therapist showed her different objects and tried to get her to name them. Some she named with nouns of her own invention. Sounds. Some she misnamed but came close – like "keys" she called "locks", "books" she called "bucks". The therapist told us she was suffering from something called Aphasia where the comprehension of language symbolism becomes jumbled. In other words, she may recognize an object but not remember the name for it. She told us this was normal and would phase itself out.

Her muscles began to get stronger. We could walk her halfway down the corridor and back with one of us on each side of her. She'd lost so much weight we could feel the bones through her arms. She seemed smaller in every respect. Fragile. Each step she took was an effort that required the whole of herself. Sometimes we had to bend down and grab the calf of one leg and move it forward. Her feet flapped out in front of her with no pretense of a destination. She was walking just for the sake of walking. Then her eyes would wander. Some reflection off a wall, a sound, someone would pass by and her head would turn, her knees would buckle. We'd get her back to bed and she'd collapse.

One day she fell forward face first on the floor and smashed her head. Someone had left her sitting alone without buckling her safety belt and she'd tried to get up to go to the bathroom. Her wrist was badly swollen from trying to stop the fall. She began to watch her hands. She would cry about her hands. She said they were old hands. They didn't belong to her. She wanted to know where her rings were. Her wedding ring. She asked if she was still married. If she was still married then where was her wedding ring? Her little finger stiffened up and she couldn't straighten it. Her hand turned black and blue at the end of the swollen wrist.

She began to eat ravenously like she'd been starved for months. She'd push whole pieces of cake into her mouth and close her eyes in an ecstasy of oral gratification. She wouldn't close her mouth when she ate and half the food came out and into her lap. Milk drooled down her neck. Mashed banana collected under her fingernails. Her hunger reached far beyond what food could offer.

The hospital recommended transferring her to a Therapy Center where they could work with her muscles. We decided to take her home instead. A physician counseled us on the pros and cons of this decision. He cautioned us that although it would be good for her to be surrounded by familiar faces it could also be devastating to the family. We had no idea what he meant.

That night we converted the dining room into a space for her. A bed in the corner. A portable toilet. A wheelchair with a service tray. A plastic wash basin. Towels. A full supply of adult pampers. We lined the mattress with black plastic and had an argument about the order of absorbent towels and sheets, trying to remember how they'd done it at the hospital. We pulled the safety belt around the mattress and I could imagine her in it. For the first time I could put myself in her place. I could feel the belt tightening across my stomach. The faces above me. The dust on the ceiling. We put flowers in the room, yellow Marguerites. We were all excited about bringing her home.

We bought her a purple knit cap and a pair of shades at Thrifty's in the morning. We brought her slippers and pajamas in a paper bag. All the nurses on the floor said goodbye to her and told her to come visit them. She said she would. They gave us her red hair wrapped in a plastic bag with her name on it. I put the bag in my pocket. It felt like a part of her still. I was suddenly seized with the superstition that her hair might fall into bad hands. That a curse could be cast on her by the possessor of her hair. I vowed to keep it in my pocket until she was out of danger.

When she first met the air outside the hospital it took her breath away. She was thrilled by every smell. The street made her smile. On the way back across the Golden Gate Bridge I asked her if she could see the sail boats way down below. She said no. Her eyes were squinting from the sun. She hadn't been in direct sunlight for over two months.

We carried her up the stairs in our arms. Her legs dangled. She giggled. The dogs were glad to see her.

That night was the beginning of the worst. She began to moan in an agonizing animal voice. We'd ask her what was the matter and she'd just moan. She'd keep it up for hours. Then she'd scream. She said she knew one of us was going to kill her. We told her it wasn't true. Not to think like that. But she was convinced one of us was trying to kill her. We asked her why she thought that and she'd say because she was "in the way". She said we'd put her in a separate room so we could "do her in". She was afraid of the night. Afraid of the sounds outside. She was afraid the dogs would eat her feet. She was afraid we'd hired someone to come and take her away. Assassins. She was afraid of being smothered by pillows. Any sudden sound. She would jump if someone turned on the water or flushed the toilet. She questioned every sound from the street. Every nail being hammered in the distance. Every saw. Car radios terrified her. She knew the pills we were giving her were going to slowly poison her. When we told her they were to help her sleep, she said they were to help her sleep "forever". She'd pretend to take them then spit them out when we weren't looking. We'd find them the next day under her bed. We began to hear ourselves the way she heard us. When we modified our voices to give her the impression of our harmlessness we heard how she took this as an ominous sign of our deep treachery. When we stood in the same room with her we tried not to assume accidental postures that she might interpret as violent. Some days every move we made was so filled with tension it was hard not to believe the role she'd cast us in was true. She began to conspire with us individually. Trying to get us to take sides against each other. Each day a different one of us was under suspicion and she'd caution us against that one. "The Traitor" is how she'd name him. We should beware of "The Traitor". We should realize that we were all in danger. Not just her. "The Traitor" would kill us all. He would wipe us out when we least expected it. We should kill "The Traitor" before he killed us.

We held council meetings late at night after she'd fallen asleep. We began arguing amongst ourselves about each one's approach to the problem. One of us was indulging her. Another was too harsh. Another one was giving her drugs behind our backs. None of us knew what to do. We took sides then shifted sides. We consulted the doctors. They recommended new drugs. Different drugs. We began having nightmares that *she* was trying to kill *us*. Images borrowed from horror films of her standing in hallways gripping butcher knives, pillows dripping with blood, blood pouring out under doorways. We never told each other these dreams until later.

One morning she asked about her mother. She wanted to

know where her mother was. When we told her she'd died a long time ago she began to cry. She cried like a baby. Her whole body would weep. Then she'd touch her scar. Run her fingers slowly down the barren skin and ask us how she got it. We told her but she didn't remember. We told her the names of the doctors. She didn't remember. We told her she was home now but she didn't remember. Her head would fold forward so that her chin rested on her breastbone. Tears flooded her knees. This posture told her whole story. She would sit slumped over like that for hours. We'd try to straighten her out but she'd fold back up again. She'd fold into herself completely. Every day she would ask us again about her mother. She would ask us if we knew for sure she was dead. She'd ask us where she was buried. How long ago. What city she died in. She couldn't believe it. For days she mourned for her mother who had died a long long time ago.

It's been exactly a year to this day. She walks on her own now. She feeds herself. She speaks with a strange accent but takes part in our conversations. She still falls silent and sits and stares into space for long periods of time. She refers to her past as the time before she was "blown away".

29/9/80
San Francisco, Ca.

Double Roses
She says

Like in England
Like back in England

And she leans way back
Inside herself
Inside of England

Her nose flares
Her eyes close
The Rose sails her home

22/9/80
San Francisco, Ca.

HAWK MOON

*A Book of Short Stories, Poems
and Monologues*

for
Patti Lee

A boy has never wept
nor
dashed a thousand kim.

Dutch Schultz

HAWK MOON MONTH

Hawk Moon month November month my birthday month month of cold set in month when secrets start whisper on the mesa high old ancient sacred land of Hopi month Antelope deer and antler clan first signs of barren empty need for prayer first dance snake in mouth dance spirit dance snake mouth painted hand and lightning bolt month of washing long black hair my month of birth month – the Hawk Moon month.

BACK IN THE 1970s

The kids prayed for a pool hall, fought hard on Friday nights right in the middle of the highway, stopping traffic. No knives, guns or chains. Just fists. Nobody was after blood. Not like city fights. The dances at Diligent River always drew a big crowd and big fights broke out between rival towns, just like back in El Monte Legion Stadium days. Boredom was the big killer. No jobs, no pool hall, ten guys to one girl and that one was usually ugly, bad radio stations, old people dying and drunk, church bazaars, one dance a month and not even Rock and Roll, one juke box that never changed its records, heavy cold snowbound winters and foggy summers. The most exciting thing that ever happened was somebody shooting a moose or a bear and that was pretty rare. Then the Americans came. First a little trickle then a whole river. Draft dodgers, criminals, escapees from the cities that were blowing up right and left. Strange pornographic literature began to circulate through the villages. Full-blown color pages of cock and pussy and tits and ass. Drugs seeped in like salty sea air. Rock and Roll hummed and blasted out of the forests drowning out the chain saws. Teepees and strangely shaped domes with glaring colors and weird designs. Long flowing ribbon banners fluttered in the fields amazing the crows. Black and chrome monster motorcycles chomped into the dirt lumber roads. Stampedes of choppers and hogs roaring through fishing villages. Rolling Stones posters pasted to the sides of barns and churches. Tattoos showing up on local girls in places you'd never think of. The Mounties were called in but things were too far gone. There was no way of telling a Canadian kid from an American. Everybody fucking and sucking and smoking and shooting and dancing right out in the open. And far off you could hear the sound of America cracking open and crashing into the sea.

THE PHANTOM TRAILER

A phantom trailer moves through the back lawns. It's been taken over by leather bandits, Mexican whores and dogs. Before that it was owned by an old couple who bought it and moved to the desert for their lungs. Now they lie without their heads in a Death Valley ditch. The driver pulls the trailer with a '56 Chevy ½-ton painted steel blue from what it used to be. He lost one eye on the horn of a six-point buck while he was trying to skin it alive. He sings in Spanish and speaks in tongues when the radio goes on the blink. In the bed of the truck is a Blue Tick Coon Hound named Jude tied by rags which she chews but can't get through 'cause she's too old and lost her teeth on buffalo bones. A little girl from Oaxaca feeds Jude with Antelope meat that she chews on for hours for the juice then spits the pulp in Jude's mouth. Inside the trailer the color TV is the center of attraction and everyone crowds around it in a half-moon shape. Because it's never been turned off day or night the sound doesn't work and the color's been distorted to bright green. Only two channels work and they both show the news but the people don't seem to care. There's one old man named Felix who never watches the news but just walks in a perfect square hugging the walls of the trailer and crossing himself with a picture of Kennedy all faded and torn in his left hand. They stop sometimes on the outskirts of town and shoot one golden spider web flare into the sky to let the High School boys know they're there. We watch from our windows on the seventh of every other month and when we see the signal we all go down in pairs, dressed in tight peggered pants and white bucks and tight T-shirts with our Camels rolled up in the shirt sleeves. We wait in the woods by the drainage ditch and sit in our '32 Fords blinking the lights on and off. Felix comes out with a flashlight and blinks us back. Then we fight for who goes first. The fights are always silent and fast because nobody wants to shoot their whole load. The losers go last but sometimes wind up the best 'cause by that time the girls are so tired that they even come and call out our names. I always got the feeling that they liked the losers best. Once me and a girl named Lupe (who was the skinniest) even came at the very same time. Just once that happened and I'll never forget. The next time the trailer came around she was gone. They told me she died in San Diego when some guy put Spanish fly in her Coke and left her in his car to go get a rubber. When he came she had the stick shift shoved so far into her womb that she bled to death.

CLAW CLOUD

He was so fat he couldn't get down off the tractor. The old John Deere just sat there popping and hissing in the green sun. The harrow stood ready, waiting with its claws to grab into the earth.

There was nothing left to do. The potatoes, the corn, the beans, the peas. Not a weed in sight. Sweat ran down into the grease and crackled on the steel. He turned the key off and the engine cranked down to a halt. Wind from the north hit him across the chops. He just sat there looking in four directions then finally to the little speck of a white house in the distance. He thought he saw a beautiful tall blonde woman come out the front door and wave for him to come in for dinner. But she vanished. Then he saw a yellow flag with a green maple leaf raise itself slowly on the flag pole and burn itself up when it hit the top. There was a cloud directly above him in the shape of a bear claw. The only claw in the sky. The only cloud. A shiver went through him but he didn't shake. It wasn't cold. He wasn't scared. Just fat and tired. He wanted to move his arms and legs. The impulse was there but nothing happened. Ducks flew in a "V". Dust rolled the smaller rocks. He looked down at his fat hands gripping the wheel like clamps as though he were still plowing. He felt the blood roaring to the surface. Something began to happen. He was turning to stone. Slowly. As hard as a rock. In his feet and hands then moving up until his whole body was petrified. He couldn't move a finger. Rooted in the earth. The claw cloud came down and scooped him up with one sweep. He rose into the air light as a ribbon. Rolled and danced and tumbled like a weed. His mouth opened wide and the wind gushed in like water. He let loose an animal sound like a great Black Bear and the whole earth shuddered. The tractor fell on its side with the front wheel spinning. The house far below snapped open its doors and the windows burst their frames. The crops uprooted and flew up like crows. By this time tomorrow he was far out over the ocean causing a tidal wave. Small ships pointed up at a strange fat black claw cloud in the sky and prayed.

BLOOD MILK

The spirit goat moved white with its long goatee and pointed horns, tied by a chain, in a circle, going in a circle, the same circle path, well worn with shit and piss by hooves. All this under a spotlight from the tar paper shack. Bugs, moths, mosquitos clumping in buzzing bunches, cracking into the glass, falling and rising in vertical lines all around the light and head of the man sitting on wooden planks with a captain's cap whittling a ship with a jacknife. She'd milked right through the winter without being bred, over a quart and a half a day. But lately the milk had started getting a pink tinge to it and in the mornings blood settled to the bottom of the bottle. The Captain didn't mind though. Once a cow he'd milked for three years straight did the same thing and the blood went away. He drank it right along. It reminded him of a strawberry milk shake. Each day the goat milk had been getting pinker though until finally it was bright red and about two thirds blood to one third milk. He kept drinking it just the same. He said it was good for the eyes. He noticed the change in the goat's pupils from day to night. How in the day the pupil narrowed down to a black horizontal slit in a yellow eye to keep out the sun's rays and at night the pupil opened all the way to let in more light. His were doing the same. He could feel it. He liked that. He liked getting close to animals that way. Learning their tricks. Feeling their souls. The goat would dance sometimes and play with the flying chips of wood that sprung from the knife. He'd talk and sing to her and cluck like a chicken. She'd baa back and a language began to set itself up. Pretty soon he'd baa three times and she'd do the same. Then she'd baa a certain number and he'd answer. Between the two creatures baaing a third voice made itself heard. They both listened. It told them to look to Venus. So they did. A light flashed and exploded in the sky but they weren't afraid. The voice came again: "Do you know where you are?" Then disappeared. They couldn't answer. And the next day the milk turned white as snow.

SLEEPING AT THE WHEEL

"Let's face it, we know very little about the total picture and that's the truth." His piss burned a hole through the thick wet pine needles. I stood around watching then took one myself, feeling a little awkward about watching. We climbed back in the old Plymouth. I was set to go but he sat there fiddling with the keys and remarking about the Redwoods. "Fuck analyzing. I mean who's the analyzer. Who's the judge. Who's the big one. There's too many in there working at once. All clanging around with their hands raised, trying to get a turn." "Right," I said. "Like this car is going to look like a prairie schooner to people fifty years from now. Say you came from another planet and landed here for a visit. Just to check things out. Where would you go first?" Not realizing this was a direct question I stared out the cracked window at a kid in a tree house throwing pine cones at a black dog. "Where would you go? Well you sure as hell wouldn't go to the back woods or some little fishing village. You'd head straight for the Big Apple. Times Square, 42nd Street. That's where you could really study the planet earth."

"Maybe we should get back to the girls," I said sort of half-assed. It seemed to work though. He slid the key in and turned her over. We rumbled off, down the mountain. "I mean every once in a while I'm just amazed when I catch a glimpse of who I really am. Just a little flash like the gesture of my hand in a con-versation and WHAM there's my old man. Right there, living inside me like a worm in the wood. And I ask myself, 'Where have I been all this time? Why was I blind. Sleeping. Just the same as being asleep. We're all asleep. Being awake is too hard.'" This set me to thinking of a story that a friend of mine from Saskatchewan once told while we were driving North on Route 96. I asked him if he'd ever been in a bad car crash and he laughed like it was some kind of joke. He said he used to get in one every week. The worst one he said was when he was driving back from someplace where he'd been drinking for two days and nights straight without any sleep. It was night time and he kept falling asleep at the wheel and shaking himself awake, slapping his face and pinching his leg till it bled. The next morning he woke up and found himself still in the car at the wheel. He opened the door to get out and put one foot out but couldn't find the ground. He looked down and saw that his car was stuck in the top of a huge oak tree about thirty feet off the ground. He looked up and saw where he'd smashed through the barricades off a bridge and people were lining up to take a look at the accident. Finally he just climbed down out of the tree, waved at the people and left the car there to rot.

"I mean where have we been all this time? What happens between the past and the future?"

"You got me," I said and settled back, pretending to be asleep.

HORSE THIEVES

Horse thieves in dark black to match the day hands and knees through crawdad brook horsefly grass brush silent signals split and circle old corral with pinto black and bay heads down munching oats switching blue blow flies closing in sliding up like old friends touch blankets flanks twitch wild eyes head up jerks and circles once then stops takes hackamore rope bit in teeth bites loose then both swing up and jump clear running wild out straight for blue space rifles blazing tongues amazed at wind and free strong power headlong into who knows where.

DAKOTA

Outside Rapid City flat blue grey Sioux plains a sign with a light old red peeled paint says see the last of the great buffalo in sawdust broken pails and crumbling corral the cow and her calf in half-moon light touched by the hand of one old man says he knew Kit Carson back when he'd shoot an Injun or two for breakfast the cow snorts flying sawdust chips the calf sucks the cars drone past going too fast to stop for a sideshow.

MONTANA

He sat there on the bed counting his money. Five thousand in cash. Mostly hundred-dollar bills. He began licking one side of the bills and pasting them with a vacant feeling on the tits of the naked corpse. He started feeling better already and covered the whole body with the bills. He'd always wanted to be a sculptor. After the girl's body was completely covered he got up and walked to one side of the room and squinted his eyes halfway like his mother taught him and took a long look at his handiwork. He moved to different parts of the room and did the same thing. He chuckled but caught himself. He walked to a desk, pulled open a drawer and drew out an old Buntline Special with an extra long barrel. He handled the gun and ran his fingers along the smooth black barrel and spun the chamber twice. He put the gun to his head and pulled the trigger. CLICK! He spun the chamber twice again and went to the girl's body. He spread her legs and slowly pushed the barrel up into her womb. He pulled the trigger again. CLICK! He withdrew the gun and spun the chamber, aimed it at the head of an owl statue and blew it apart. The bullet

132

hit the plaster wall with a thud. He fell on the floor laughing. He struggled to gain control of himself. Now was no time to go off the deep end. He finally stopped his hysterical laughter and lay very still staring up at the ceiling. He began to very slowly put himself through some Yoga positions. He'd been noticing how his flow of blood was slowing down. First he did the Plow for about five minutes. Then the Cobra. Then a head stand. Then the Lion. Then a few breathing exercises. After this he began to feel the blood flowing freely and felt refreshed again. He got up off the floor, shook himself like a dog and walked to the closet. He opened it and pulled out his favorite cowboy gear: Kangaroo skin boots in white with red flower designs and a high riding heel. Big rawhide chaps with fringe and silver Navajo studs. A black satin Gene Autry shirt with white pistols embroidered on the collar and cuffs. His favorite bright orange Roy Rogers bandana. His Lone Ranger mask. And a black stetson hat with a chin string. Finally he pulled out the golden spurs with silver chains and leather straps. He laid them all out on the floor in the right order so they looked like the shape of a man. The Super Cowboy Man. Then he took off all his clothes and walked naked to the window of the hotel. He opened the french window and walked out on to the terrace. The wind hit him cold but the sun was still out. He stared up 23rd Street to the East River and the Con Ed chimneys with their red rings around the top. Then down 23rd to the Hudson. He breathed the wind and looked down seven stories at the little people then across to the YMCA where the Indians were having a pow-wow. His legs were getting goose bumps so he jumped back inside and closed the window. He stopped and looked again at the naked body covered with money. Then at the cowboy shape on the floor. He walked over and picked up the shirt and put it on. Then the chaps. Then the boots. Then the spurs. Then the bandana. Then the hat. Then the mask. He stood up and walked to the mirror. He picked up the gun and did a few twirling and fast draw tricks then stuck the barrel inside the waist of his chaps. He was well pleased with what he saw. Now what?

He'd like to go down to the bar for a drink. A Scotch and soda or a bourbon or something. First he should turn on some music so the neighbors wouldn't know he was out. He picked out the *Sticky Fingers* album and put it on the stereo full volume then left the room. He could still hear 'Wild Horses' all the way down the elevator. It gave him a good feeling. Like someone was taking care of her while he was gone. He got to the bar and sat down next to a man who'd had his voice larynx thing removed so he had to talk through a plastic tube which made him sound like a transistor radio. The baseball game was on and the Spanish waiters were complaining about the Espresso machine and how the steam burned them all the time. He watched the game for a while but baseball always bored him. Stock car racing was his favorite sport aside from the rodeo. He turned to the man with the voice box and asked him if he knew anything about cremation. The man was a little shocked by the mask and the question but said something about pouring gasoline over the body very lightly in order to save all the ashes. So he finished his double tequila, paid the bill and went outside for a cab. He headed straight for "Joe's Friendly Service" in the Village. His favorite gas station because it was so old and run by a Swede who loved New York. He asked Joe for a gallon of super octane in a can and left a deposit then hopped back in a cab and drove back to the hotel. All the way up the elevator he could hear 'Moonlight Mile' coming loud and clear from his room. He walked in and there she was, still covered with the money, still sleeping forever. He set down the can of gas, walked to the bed and lifted her up and carried her into the bathroom. Hundred-dollar bills floated to the floor and fell from her tits. He set her down softly in the cold bathtub with most of the money still clinging to her skin. He opened the can of gas and sprinkled it lightly along her legs, over her waist and chest and head and hair. Then he bent down slowly and kissed her on the lips. The taste of gas in his mouth made him feel like hitting the road. He struck a match and tossed it on the body. The bills burst into flame and then caught her skin. Her body went up like a torch. The skin crackled and popped and turned black under the bright orange rage. The body twisted from the heat and turned to one side. He could almost see her eyes through the flaming licks. He stood there cold and empty for a long time until the fire died and smoke rose in little curls. Then he turned the shower on and watched the ashes spin down the drain leaving nothing but bones and teeth on the white porcelain. He shut the shower off, pulled the curtain and walked back into the room. He picked up four hundred-dollar bills off the floor and stuck them in his shirt pocket. He put the needle on 'Sister Morphine' and walked out the door leaving it wide open. All the way down the elevator he could hear the song. He went straight through the lobby, threw his key on the desk and walked out to hail a cab. A big yellow Checker drew up. He swung in with his spurs jangling and said: "Montana, please."

HEAVEN'S FIST

Far shooting star
Scar branded night
Car light snakes a trail
On earth
Far far heaven's head
Opens up its bony skull
Shows a flash of secret sight
Then fast the fist slams shut

LONG TALL SALLY

Cool and weary
Tongue tied down
Back strapped to a wind mill
Round and round
Long Tall Sally
In the alley
Caught and taken
For a witch

SPIRIT

Spirit
With a wet nose
Lump on the neck
Sits in corners of my room
Says not to fear
Breaks the windows to breathe
Then leaves
Like that

STRANGER

I keep waking up in whoever's
Body I was last with
Who's this
Arms like a Viking
Rolled bull muscles
Hair down to here
I'm enough of a stranger as it is

DEMON'S TEST

I couldn't believe I was all alone. Puking lobster into a bucket and carrying it outside in the dark. Dumping it where the fox would probably find it. Carrying it back in and trying to sleep. Knowing there were ghosts. Hearing the fog horn. Watching the night swallows bashing into the window. Praying for morning and sun and happy thoughts. What a night. I remember a prayer that went: "Great human wild animals. Keep watch over them." And I started to talk it, then sing it to myself, then out loud to the blackness. I kept up the chant, doing it first in Soul rhythms, then Calypso, then Country Western, then Rolling Stones, then waltz time, then back to Soul. As I did this I opened a Moose Head beer and guzzled and paced the house. Whenever I got the urge to vomit I'd sing the prayer harder and louder and almost angry against the demon. I couldn't make out his shape but I knew him from a long time ago. His face was grey and long. He kept wanting me to change the song, to change the rhythms, to pick up knives and slash myself but I kept away. I sang the prayer in his face. I'd sweat and tremble when he touched me. I never begged. I fought. I bit his finger off and spit it down the stairs. He screamed and pushed me after it. I hit the floor and rolled. I rolled with every punch, protecting my kidneys and groin. I sang as I rolled. I crawled into the kitchen and lay face down on the floor. He changed his shape to small crawling things of the dust and skittered across my back making pin hole teeth marks in my neck. "Great human wild animals! Keep watch over them! Keep watch over them!" He pulled me out on to the porch by my arms and kicked at my head. I ran to the alders and hid. I could hear him coming like a snake. I ran for the open fields but fell and lay still in the couch grass. The moon moved faster than the clouds. The race was on. I pulled myself up and got to a gulley where the marsh began. He was on me again. Slashing at my back. I slid to the bottom and sank in putrid smelling water. I covered myself in the stuff and half swam the best I could. Like a dog sinking in a lake. He gurgled behind. I sang at the night. The spring peepers answered me and made me strong. Strong enough to win. I made it to the beach and ran straight into the ocean up to my waist and stopped. The freezing water brought me to my senses. This was the test. To go straight ahead and never come back or to turn back now. I stayed like that until morning singing my song. When the sun came the bottom half of me was frozen stiff, the top half was warm.

GUADALUPE IN THE PROMISED LAND

Guadalupe hit the skids and fishtailed into a ditch, crawled out of the wreck bleeding from the neck, saw the moon, laid his head in a mud puddle, said, "Todo el Mundo" three times and snuffed out. Him and Manolete got together after that and Manolete told him it wasn't enough just to be a man. The thing to shoot for was sainthood. He said he almost hit it. A saint of the cape. Jackson Pollock joined them and told Manolete he was full of shit. A man was good enough. That was harder than sainthood. There's too many saints anyway. Guadalupe didn't know what to think. He ran into Jimmy Dean and Jimmy just looked confused. Marilyn Monroe had no opinion. Brecht kept talking about Germany and shame. Satchmo kept wiping his sweat and shuffling. Janis wanted more. Crazy Horse said: "Fight and die young." Brian Jones just played the harpoon. Dylan Thomas said: "Rage." Jimi Hendrix said: "Slide." Bip Bopper said: "What?" Johnny Ace said: "Shoot." And Davey Moore said "Take it all on." That made sense to Guadalupe. And with that he lay down for a nice long rest.

DESERTED

Fangs out it lunged for meat and cracked its head on the glass. Fell back, belly up in a tropical miniature garden. Like a nine-hole pitch and putt minus the pitchers. Squirming, flopping over, right side up and panting, sides heaving, scales swelling and falling, cracking off like paint. Begins to move and slide in a sideways shuffle through the moss and fern and finds a white mouse, swallows it whole like a fly and keeps on going. Avoids a giant pink-fingered tentacle hand with bitten-off nails and axle grease and black and blue thumb. Runs right into another one and silently screams, slashes with teeth and claws but is caught firm around the midriff and hoisted like a plane over six feet in the air. Then set down suddenly and left in a giant open-air arena with no glass forever and stars for lights and moon for more. Miles and miles of this going on and on. The sound of the tentacled one's car fading off in the distance. Can't move. Frozen with vastness and uncertainty. The silent boom of desert. Deserted. Left to be wild and not knowing how any more. Not needing to be. It slowly eats its tail and hind legs and belly and swallows itself whole. In the morning a truck roars by without a driver, the radio blaring. Just the truck, the radio and the desert.

WIPE OUT
(To be read while listening to 'Wild Horses')

After playing *Wipe Out* all day and all night for three full days without stopping even to snort some coke or rest his calluses, Cobra Moonstar fell on top of his Les Paul Gibson and broke his nose. He didn't care. It felt good. More good honest pain. The little Fender Princeton amp buzzed and sputtered like a '32 Ford, the tubes flickering golden light like the morning coming up. Cobra's stomach growled like feedback. The garbage trucks were starting up their crunching grinding. Cobra thought of Dylan's *New Morning* and knew what it "meant". He let out a long fart that smelled like "Good and Plenty" since that's all he'd been eating before he went on his fast. He wished he had a woman around to make a coke run or massage his back or give him some head or just talk about something like early Yardbirds or just rub his head or something. He couldn't feel his fingers. His ears were buzzing, throbbing with electric waves. The floor felt good. The guitar was a little uncomfortable as a pillow but nothing mattered

like that. His animal spirit was king. He'd cracked through. Now
he had his chops. Now he'd earned his half-moon tattoo on his
left hand and his pierced ear. The blood from his nose was
forming a little river. He watched it run across the floor heading
straight for his collection of old 45s. He licked it and lapped it up
like a puppy. Nice and salty. The crab lice he'd picked up from a
Vogue model he'd balled twice last week were starting to wake
up in their pubic nest. He didn't care. It tickled a little but he was
too tired to scratch. Their movement was even kind of exciting.
Like friends saying good morning. Friendly. He felt his balls
moving around, shifting position. His joint started swelling. He
remembered how embarrassed he used to get when he was a kid
and he'd get a hard-on from petting his dog. Trying to hide the
bulge in his crotch. Digging around in his pockets and shifting
the position of his cock so it stood straight up and laid flat against
his belly. Now he didn't care. He laughed at his old self like it was
another person. His joint grew hard and strong now and reached
out for food like a baby bird's neck. How come now when he was
so tired and wasted? He could call up Sheila or Mabelline but he
didn't really want to fuck. An orgasm would be nice but not all
the lovemaking preparation, undress, "Do you love me?" stuff.
Just to come would be nice. "You can't always get what you
want," he thought candidly. The guitar sure felt good now. He
licked the Super Slinkies and remembered Jimi Hendrix in the
old days. He licked some more on the strings surprised at the
similarity in taste of the steel to the taste of pussy. His tongue ran
up and down. Maybe it was the combination of blood and steel.
Like bleeding pussy. Nice. Even the smell. His joint was throbbing now. Blood rushing. Even a tingle like the real thing. He
tried to fantasize a beautiful chick like Brigitte Bardot or Anna
Karina or Tuesday Weld but they didn't seem to matter. The
Gibson was good enough. She was turning the trick. He
unzipped and yanked it out rubbing it between the volume
knobs. With each stroke his cock made the Gibson howled. The
volume knob rolling with the strokes. This was really something.

He was really getting it on. The guitar seemed to dig it too. The harder he pumped the more she screamed. The more she screamed the harder he pumped. He ripped at the strings with his teeth. The E string snapped and whipped across his face. His tongue ran up and down the neck getting at all the frets. His hands reached out for the amp and caught hold. Just as he came a bolt of electric shock struck through him like lightning. His hands turned blue. His hair jumped out straight and turned white. He screamed with the Gibson and came all over her. Long stringy white lumps of rushing come gushing and gushing like boiling over pudding. His whole body went stiff, taut like a bow. Then it was over. He fell limp and rolled over on his back panting and gasping for air. He just lay there staring up at the ceiling for a long time. Then he laughed. "If you try sometimes you can get what you need," he thought matter-of-factly.

SILENT STAMPEDE

Night moss marsh in moose in flesh grass marsh wet strings of reeds and hooves in mud track beach track tractor track sound of chain saw ripping bark rip tree rip moose run herds and herds stampede the white village through the church bloody priest antler gash and rip down store and walls all hell breaks loose the Eskimo Ice Age old age old age weather summer fall spring ice break ice breaker North shake earth shake day shake night shake star shake day break light and sound off pole off bounce and splinter quakes and shifts the poles earth axis earth hemispheres and balls and spheres and globes and knots and nuts and bolts hold together holding holding screws and nuts break holds bust loose off balance tip and twist turn ripping sideways shifting Moon for Venus turn and turn the secret Venus turn hand Venus secret silent secret silent turning Moon Venus silent secret silent secret Earth.

CAN A ½-TON FLY?

Green Moon scraped the cow shit off his boots and bent down to smell it, stuck his finger in it, wiped it off on his shirt tail, shuffled to the stove and threw a log on, knocked over a pint of whiskey and growled, got down and licked it up, pulled a splinter out of his tongue and punched his fist through the side of the cardboard shack. He stood there drunk and dazed with his arm half inside and half outside. He felt the difference in the weather outside and in. Then he punched his other fist through and felt what that was like. Same thing. When Skunk Tails arrived in the ½-ton Green Moon was still like that, both his hands and half his arms sticking through. Skunk Tails grabbed a piece of rope from the bed of the truck and snuck up on the hands. He quickly grabbed Green Moon's arms and pulled them tight then wrapped the rope around both wrists and tied a square knot so there was no escape. Skunk Tails giggled and went back to the truck, hauled out a six-pack and some bourbon and went into the shack. Green Moon was unconscious on the floor with his arms still stuck up in the wall. He looked like a slaughtered lamb. Skunk Tails giggled some more, opened a can of beer and poured it over Green Moon's head. That brought him around but he couldn't figure out how come his arms were stuck through the wall. Skunk Tails giggled and Green Moon let out a bellow like a bull moose and pulled half the wall of the shack down. He lay on the floor with his hands still tied. The hole in the wall let in the cool night and you could see all the lights down in Yellow Knife. Green Moon was really pissed off by this time because Skunk Tails just sat there and giggled, guzzling beer and slapping his knee. Green Moon rolled around on the floor, crashing into the stove, biting at his wrists and pounding his head on the floor. Finally Skunk Tails stood up, took out his jackknife and cut him loose. Green Moon tackled him to the floor, grabbed the knife away and slashed Skunk Tails across the knee. Skunk Tails just laughed and poured bourbon all over the wound. Then Green Moon laughed and took a long pull on the bottle. They both sat there on the floor staring out the hole in the wall at the lights reflecting off the water. They decided to go down and pick up their friend Fox Hand and take a drive through the town. Fox Hand was busy frying Caribou eyes but he left them burning and joined his friends. They drove for a while through every street and alleyway in Yellow Knife, singing and pounding on the dash-board. Green Moon went unconscious again. The town was dead and buried. Fox Hand suggested they go across the draw bridge and look at the lights from the other side of the river.

On the other side of the river was a car full of tourists waiting patiently for a ship to pass under the bridge. The iron tongues of the draw bridge began to rise slowly up into the sky. The bell was ringing and red lights blinked on and off. The ship slowly slid its way up to the slot. The tourists watched an old gray $\frac{1}{2}$-ton pull up on the other side and stop. One of them said: "Those look like Indians." Another one said: "Could be, or Eskimos maybe." Then they watched the $\frac{1}{2}$-ton start up again and move half way up the rising bridge. One of the tourists gasped and clutched a hand to her chest. "They must be crazy!" But the $\frac{1}{2}$-ton stopped again. The ship moved closer and nudged its nose into the opening. The $\frac{1}{2}$-ton started up again and moved straight up to the top of the rising tongue and plunged straight off into thin air. The tourists screamed as they watched the truck smash against the bow of the ship and plunge into the river sending up huge green gurgling bubbles. The ship went on, the draw bridge closed and the car full of tourists drove back to where they came from.

SEVEN IS A NUMBER IN MAGIC

Seven nurses still dressed in white standing on a cement island in the night with yellow flashing lights causing cars to skirt the island, out late after a night on the town and drunk laughing, telling jokes about the handsome doctor, the ugly old man with the leaking bladder, the psychosomatic lady with serum hepatitis and the cars picking up their skirts and wolf whistles aimed at their legs, without fear of any danger in the air, just the city fun of being young and free after working hours.

Seven twelve-year-old kids riding beat up customized Schwinns and stolen bikes with racoon tails flying from the handle bars and raised up seats and little wheels in front and big ones in the back and high risers and mud flaps with red and orange reflectors and the Ace of Spades stuck in their spokes come riding up and form a circle around the seven nurses closing in and making sounds of cats in heat. At first the nurses laugh and make "Oh brother!" faces at each other then they try to move on down the street to a place with more light and more people walking by. But the kids close the circle in and start to wave silver car antennas like whips in their faces and call out Spanish names which the nurses catch the meaning of. Now the panic starts and the nurses cry out for what they want and the kids say to dump their purses out in the middle of the island. The first one says no and gets a slash across the face with the silver whip. She screams and gets another slash. One of the smart ones dumps her purse first and the others follow suit until a big mound of lipstick, wallets, perfume, tissues, Tampax, coins and bills, stamps, hairpins, false fingernails and polish, hair spray, pictures of lovers, powder puffs, and files lie strewn across the pavement. The kids ride through it with their bikes, crushing and smashing all the stuff and grabbing handfuls of money with their teeth the way cowboys do at the rodeo. The stupid nurse who screamed tries to make a run for it across the street and one of the kids with

145

"El Corason" written across the back of his purple silk jacket rides after her, doing wheel stands and burning rubber right on her heels. She falls like a calf and the kid leaps off his bike, pulls a switchblade and cuts off her left ear. He turns and raises it high to his comrades, dripping with blood and stuck on the tip of the knife. They call out "Olé!" and ride off with the kid with the ear in the lead.

The next day the six nurses bring the seventh one with one ear a transistor radio to her room in the hospital where she used to work. They all make jokes about at least she knows what she's in for.

The kid with the nurse's ear sits on top of a roof on his haunches staring down at the ear. He drives a hole through the white lobe with a nail and threads it on a leather thong then puts it around his neck. He stands up and raises a fist to the sky. The Gods are well pleased.

WHO WOULD'VE THOUGHT

Who would've thought the English would cop our music. Who would've thought our music would cop the world. Who would've thought Africa would cop America. Who would've thought the Indians would cop the French. Who would've thought Brecht would cop Dylan's mind. Who would've thought that time was on our side.

HOLLYWOOD

The cowboy dressed in fringe with buckskin gloves, silk bandana, pale clown white make-up, lipstick, eyes thickly made up and a ten-gallon hat, holds the reins of his horse decked out in silver studs. The cowboy squints under hot spotlights. The gaffers all giggle. The cowboy sweats but there's nowhere for the sweat to go. He sinks to his knees and screams: "Forgive me, Utah! Forgive me!"

GUAM

A jeep bounces violently through lush jungle green hanging wet dripping plants with snakes. The mother fires four shots from her revolver out the window through the thick rain, the kid on the floor in a cowboy hat covering his ears. The Japs run for cover in loincloths and sneakers, one bleeding from the side, and hide in caves. The jeep crashes on through to black sticky asphalt and the ride smoothes out. She sticks the gun back under the seat and pats the kid on the head. They arrive at the drive-in theatre and stop, plug in the speaker and sit back to watch *Song of the South*.

SWEAT SAINT

Down in the sweat pit. The leaders have told me to stay until my vision comes. I sweat it out for days. "I'm not a visionary!" I keep screaming. Bashing my head with stones. The old men come in once a day and pour cold water on the hot stones then leave the place looking like LA on the worst smoggy day. I hack my way through the steam to the bolted door and call out for "at least a cheeseburger!" but they're long gone. My stomach jumps like a frog. "How can torture bring you peace! I'm just a dish washer, not a warrior!" They already have plans for my marriage to the ugliest girl on the block. My uncle Buzz is giving her father six black Ford Mustangs and a Castro Convertible for the deal. The trouble is I used to like her when we first moved in but now I can't stand the publicity. I keep waiting for a sign but nothing comes but sweat and hunger. Not even imagination. I go over and over the possibilities in my head: "I'll go along with the whole thing. Play dumb. Marry the chick and go on our honeymoon. Then I'll ditch her. But then they'd send their best scouts and find me. Bring me back and humiliate me in front of the whole block. Maybe even make me do the Sun Dance. I couldn't stand that. The pain. More pain! I can't stand the pain. No. I'll die like a man. I'll lie and tell the old men that I've finally had a vision. They'll let me out and take me to the Moon Dreamer. Then I'll tell him I lied and that I don't wanna marry that stupid girl. Then they'd kill me. They'd stone me to death like the Tasavuh." There's too much at stake. There's too much confusion in here. And I'm the only one. How can that be. There must be some way out. I've tried digging but the place is surrounded by Malamutes and Huskies. I wouldn't stand a snowball's chance in hell of making it to the woods without being ripped apart. If I could only disappear. If I could just sweat myself away. That's it! If I concentrate I could probably do it. I could probably just turn myself into a pool of sweat on the floor. The old men would come in and I'd be gone. A miracle they'd say. They'd celebrate the day each year by having drag races and roping off the main streets. Block dances and parties and Mardi Gras parades in honor of a Saint. A Sweat Saint. Firework displays and rodeos and ox pulls and dog races and art shows and costume balls and swimming meets and football games. All for me and my memory. But now the pit is getting muddy. The clay walls are cracking from the heat. My skin and the walls. My sweat and the mud. My breath and the steam. My head and the stones. My bones are going soggy and outside the drums have already started up.

BLACK BEAR RUG

I keep seeing a black bear rug in front of my face
Wherever I go it stares back at me
In Horn and Hardardts
There it is
I see myself sitting before it on a wooden floor
Smoking a pipe
Eskimo still
Listening to the Huskies outside ripping into their fish
It doesn't speak
It wants nothing from me
It doesn't seem at all dead though
Even though it's just the skin and fur and head and claws
And beady black berry eyes
It seems pathetic and strong
It won't answer when I ask its name
I threaten it with a Bowie Knife and all it does is grin
I take it for walks in the moonlight and it just drags its ass
I take it fishing and hunting but it doesn't care
I try to fuck it from every angle
Give it head
Up the ass
It won't have any of it
So tonight I threw it in the fire
The stink was awful
All that's left is the claws
I wear them around my neck
I wear them wherever I go
I'm real lonely for that bear

DREAM BAND

Rattle. A plane flash. Baby whimper. The house moans. The droning plane. Birds play. My tattoo itching. Anne Waldman. New Jersey. Long Island. Michael's lungs. Black spot from the Midwest. Eddie Hicks. LouEllen. All their Babies. Miners in the cave shaft. Murray and his Cheyenne headband. His grey Mustang rusted out. Feet, hands. Lubricating sweat glands. The body's secret machine. Patti and the Chelsea. David making rhubarb wine. His new camera. Scott and Annie. Their black roof. Jeeps in four-wheel drive. Sand and beach. Endless. Rattle. Wisdom teeth. Bleeding gum flap. Hydrogen Peroxide. The Beach Boys. Duarte High. John and Scarlet. Kristy and the old man who gave her presents. The Sierra Madre mountains. The Arizona border. Dylan in shades. The ship. The missile. Rattle.

THE CURSE OF THE RAVEN'S BLACK FEATHER

"Drive you fool. Up under the dashboard. Checkin' out the fuses. For a man who knows nothin' about cars but memorized the rear ends of every Chevy from 1950 to '59 you do pretty good. You're not in competition that's for sure."

You know the way a person can get in your head and stick there and roll around and you start to think about all his good points and then his bad ones and then just about him as a person? Well that's what I'm thinking about Keith Richard.

That's the thing about driving a distance, especially if you're alone. Driving alone is mainly just sitting and moving with the road. A stationary kind of act but the car keeps moving while you sit still and your feet fall asleep. Your mind races like the engine, a camera gone wild, but your body stays put. That's the thing about driving.

The thing about Keith is his shark tooth ear ring, his hawk face and his name. Not Richards but Richard. Keith Richard, two first names. "You got the silver, you got the gold. You got the diamonds from the mine." And he kicked some Scotch guy in the teeth from the stage in the early days when they played in Scotland before jeering crowds.

Some smell from the floor boards sneaks up on me like burning rubber then changes to sweet maple syrup smelling. It's funny 'cause when it smells like burning rubber I get worried and tense and wonder if we'll make it. When it changes to maple sugar I relax and feel real good about bein' back on the road. On the road, on the road, on the road.

A shooting pain through my stomach. Jack Kerouac died like that. French Canadian. I'm heading for Canada. Home of Jack. His stomach burst and bled from lush. I haven't touched a drop in three days. Maybe I need a drink. Some Navy Rum. 151 proof. Enough to kill a horse.

"It's just about a moonlight mile down the road." Down the road, down the road, down the road.

Visions of wrecks. Visions of wrecked stars; Jayne Mansfield's severed head. Jackson Pollock. Jimmy Dean. Visions of wrecked cars. Asleep at the wheel. Shaking head. Broken line. Yellow line. Solid line. Solid white line. Broken white line. Broken bones. Broke down. Stranded. Hitching for gas. Hitching in the dark. Stranded. Headlight. Searchlight. Spotlight. Flashing light. Night light. The little glowing blue ember in the kid's room to keep away the Boogie Man. Carburetors, spark plugs, generators, regulators, internal combustion, power of steel. The iron horse. But that's a train.

KEITH standing alone, outside in the California night. Standing in his Python boots staring at a kidney shaped pool. The kind Brian died in. Staring at the water. The air blowing his crow feather hair.

A RAVEN! A dead black bird hit on the wing! I slam to a stop, jump out and pluck a long plume for luck. The corpse jumps from being plucked. I jump back in and shove the feather behind the sun visor. It sticks out black. I drive and think of a movie called *The Raven* where everybody in the movie keeps saying the stuffed Raven in the movie is a symbol of death. I wonder about that. I begin to wonder. Am I going to die? Is everything a sign? "Soft Shoulder". Is everything a sign? Is it bad luck to take a dead Raven's feather? Is it diseased? From the touch of the feather. Could I die from the touch? Could I crash? I slam to a stop and run down a steep bank to a brook of clear water and wash the hand that touched the feather. I watch the curse wash away. I'm clean again. I get back in but the feather's still there. I can't touch it again or the curse won't never leave. I drive and drive like being chased. Running away.

DESTINATIONS: From some place to some place. But in between is where the action is.

The feather speaks! I'm sure of it. It has a voice. Its own peculiar voice. More like a Myna bird than a Raven. No, more like a "Nevermore" Edgar Poe Raven voice. It doesn't matter. The character is too distinct to describe. It has a voice. It definitely speaks to me. It speaks low and soft like a feather should. It mumbles with the pistons then stands out clear. Then shouts. Then lies quiet. I wait, thinking maybe I should rest. Maybe I should sleep in the back seat. Maybe it'll go away when the sun comes. Maybe. But no. The voice says this:

"Notice the way the moon beam shining on the water chases you. Chases you. As though you were the only one. No escape. I'm taking you to a special place."

"Me? Look, I'm sorry I took your feather but I thought you wouldn't mind. I mean you were dead and everything."

"My body on the asphalt. My claws. My feathers speak. My bones. My feathers speak."

"I know. Why is that? I can't figure that one out."

"It's not for you to figure. Just follow. I'll show you the way."

"But I have a date in Canada. I'm late already."

"I'll take you there then let you go."

"Where? Take me where?"

"South."

"But I'm heading North."

"Not any more."

And sure enough the signs were reading "South 201" and "South 306" and South and South and South. And how was I to know what to believe. So I went along with it. I couldn't fight it anyway. Once I tried turning around and going the opposite direction but the signs still read "South" and "South" and "South". So I was going South against my will all on account of a feather. I began to realize that part of the problem was no radio. Not having a radio was probably causing me to hear things in the air that weren't even there. If only I had me a radio. So I stopped at a radio shop and bought one. A small black Panasonic. But all that came out was the voice of the Crow. The voice of the Raven's black feather urging me on. Softly flying me South.

"You'll take me to a town called Noir in Louisiana. You'll drive straight through the town to the outskirts where you'll find a dump. A car dump full of wrecked cars. You'll park and get out of your car and walk to an old black 1936 Pontiac sitting alone off to one side. You'll get in on the driver's side and open the glove compartment. Inside you'll find six black feathers just like mine. You'll put my feather in the glove compartment with the others and close it. Then get back in your car and you're on your way."

"That's all? That's all you want me to do?"

"That's all."

153

Keith and Mick. Like brothers. Like evil sisters in disguise. The left and right hand. A two-headed beast. The music and the words. The background and the foreground. The opposite of Paul and John. The dark and the light. I've always been pulled toward darkness. Toward black. Toward death. Toward the South. Good. Now I'm heading the right direction. Away from the quaint North. Away from lobsters and white churches and Civil War graveyards and cracker-barrel bazaars. Toward the swamps, the Bayou, the Cajuns, the cotton mouth, the Mardi Gras, the crocodile.

For days I went on like this. Never stopping. Driving day and night. But they seemed the same. The dialogue never stopping. And the car kept going. I never stopped for gas even. And the car kept going. And the Crow stopped talking. I even started asking it directions but it never answered. Just some friendly conversation but it never answered. Finally I hit a town named Noir in Louisiana. I wasn't surprised. I drove straight through to the car dump and stopped. I took the feather and got out and found the old Pontiac. I got in and opened the glove compartment and laid the feather down with the six other black feathers and closed the glove compartment door. I sat there for a while just frozen. Expecting more directions I guess. No answer. I looked through the cracked glass. Nothing. I played with the wheel for a while and diddled the gear shift. I looked down and there was an old rusted key in the ignition. Not thinking I reached down and turned the key. The old engine turned right over and barked. I wasn't surprised. I put her in reverse and backed up through the piles of smashed metal and glass then drove straight out on to the highway. Straight North. I've been driving for years like that. Just North. Always going North and getting nowhere. Never stopping for gas or food or sleep or friendship. Just driving. North.

¼ MILE

Race pass blue on asphalt blue and orange lightning bolt of glass
splintered cam shaft reeled and rimmed and hooked to the left
and left in smoke and blue and blue and gone gone far asphalt
ground to meat and steel and blue and blue and ground crowd
cheer hook of cheer and plague of cheer of ask for more and more
and ground in glass smash of steel cold and blue and blue and
chants of more of more of bulls of blue of bulls of ground of
ground in blood of flood of wave of drown of rave of rage of rave
of cave of seat of crash helmet strapped in blue lightning rod of
orange and blue like Rams in blue and crash and crash and
leather smash on smash on smash on and on.

MILE AND A ¼

Hoof and turf class horse flash and green and lean and little
jockey seat hot walker trot and gate flash steel gate bell ring ring
car off-track betting with Italian gangster mobster ring in blood in
barber shop where Anastasia got his flash steel stirrup cold bet in
the pari mutuals the killing was made for gold for gold for silver
gold and python boots and hookers toots and Cadillac waits and
sits and tracks sleep sleep in hay and mangers dogs and circles of
smoke camp talk of Derby Louisville the Downs down leather
strapped to horse flesh smell of horse hair sweat and fetlock hoof
and bit and bridle chomp and bell rings bell the gate of Hell opens
to the dirt fresh harrowed by the mule team skinners from your
South where black wears black and numbers in your paper
Herald paper numbers fill your Times and gold and silver slivers
clang and clang and chime to church where the mobsters pray for

St Jude saint saints a saints day parade a bullet through the back and dead and bang goes the colt from California on his setting pace bang again he come from comes from bay black and bay tan and black mane tail and doesn't know little does he know the murder outside the mile and a quarter.

MR AND MRS SIZZLER

A yellow-and-green balsa-wood glider like an old Russian Mig hangs by a rubber band from a holly bush under Christmas lights by the front porch of a home in the Hollywood Hills. It weaves and bobs, springing like, on the rubber band from a gentle breeze. Night's just coming in. The smog's lifting. Out back the smell of T-bone steaks sizzling over open coals with the fat dripping down and popping. White German Shepherds play – fight and roll down the long green rolling lawn bumping their heads on rain birds and yipping. Dark-tan kids toss a yellow and black plastic ball back and forth in the heated pool with underwater lights shining through the pale blue chlorined water and a dead moth floating near the drain. The father stands staring into the barbecue with a long fork in one hand and wearing a long white apron with the words "Mr Sizzler" printed in red across the front. A big Boeing 747 flies over low with yellow and blue lights flashing, heading toward the LA Airport. "Mr Sizzler" looks up and remembers World War II. "Mrs Sizzler" comes out of sliding glass doors, walks across the flagstone patio with her arms folded across her chest and a cashmere sweater thrown over her shoulders. They both stand there silently staring into the red coals. Just the sound of the kids and the dogs and splashes in the pool. Then BLAM! the house blows up.

BOREDOM

Boredom was on. For dinner they ate the porkypine and shot the shit and rattled through the license plate collection, telling a different story for each state. Arkansas: "How the bear almost got Hodie". Wyoming: "The different ways they fold their hats". Mississippi: "The mongoloid idiot with the mud skiff". Two of them went off with a gallon of white gas to blow up the beach. Two more drew a circle on the wall and threw fishing knives. Two examined Venus and talked about the Hopi prophecy. The seventh stared at the mouse shit and wished for a gun. Any gun. A blue gun. A fast gun. A slow gun. A gun fight. A good fast gun fight. A Winchester, lever action 30.30. Now there's a gun to take care of anything. They look good too. Make you feel good to hold one. Like a cowboy again. Somebody was asking him to wash the dishes. He got up and broke the chair over their back. Somebody else wanted to know why he did that. He said he was dreaming of guns.

RIP IT UP

Drum bass the ghost pedal sizzle ride cymbal top hat old dixieland New Orleans way of putting it driving a band of hill billies into rock hard rock soul rhythm and blues a fight between the lead guitar and the piano player for volume the guitar wins natch the inside workings of a band the audience never sees the constant difference between the inside and the out the performer and the performance the experience and what they experience Rock and Roll is definitely a motherfucker and always will be Rock and Roll made movies theatre books painting and art go out the window none of it stands a chance against The Who The Stones and old Yardbirds Credence Traffic The Velvet Underground Janis and Jimi and on and on the constant frustration of the other artists to keep up to the music of our time Rock and Roll will never die but what about the novel the theatre and all that culture stuff Norman Mailer insisting on being a man Edward Albee working from dawn to dusk for Broadway Peter Townshend says Rock and Roll is the perfect medium for self-destruction and he don't mean suicide Joe Cocker said if he hadn't started singing he probably would have killed somebody what other art can come close to that the dancer trapped in form the actor trapped by the script Rock and Roll gets it on better than football baseball even boxing because how many knockouts or knockdowns or TKOs do you see in a fight one if you're lucky and even then it's usually down on one knee every time I saw The Who in the early days it was like watching Sonny Liston hit the canvas from start to finish the whole place going up in smoke Rock and Roll is violence manifest without hurting no one except an occasional kick in the teeth or punch in the mouth Rock and Roll is more revolutionary than revolution fuck James Taylor and all them sweethearts of the guitar pick ballad school gimmee hard ass shit kickin' music like 'Hey Joe' and 'Down Home Girl' and 'Summertime Blues' the way The Who did it Chuck Berry's 'School days' Little Richard Otis and Booker T. and Jerry Lee ROCK AND ROLL ROCK AND ROLL ROCK AND ROLL ROCK AND ROLL ROCK AND ROLL "We're gonna rock it up we're gonna rip it up and ball tonight."

ANGEL AND THE CROW BAIT

The motion animal breaks down
A little at a time
Broken horse time
Gelding with swollen fetlocks
Hoof rot from standing in the marsh grass too many days
The winged animal begins to swing in lower circles
Not looking for prey
Just praying not to crash
In Science talk it's called entropy
In Whiskey talk the shakes
In Dope talk the turkey
In Murder the heart
In Poker the bluff
In Mexico the shits
Out here we don't speak its name
We know it by the look in the fire
Angel feeds on Mule Meat and don't think about the body
He buries himself to sleep
I have to dig him out every morning
By night the dust leaves him shining
Venus combs him clean
To disappear he smears his nose in charcoal and drops
his ear ring in the frying pan
I save it for him
We meet up in a Gallup Pawn Shop
He trades the ring for an Eagle claw on a leather thong
He makes me pierce his nose with a hot toothpick
The claw hangs down over his black teeth
He's happy now
To celebrate we steal a jukebox and take it down to the dump
It plays all night on good faith

A red Coyote wants to dance but Angel scares him off with the
claw
And I'm getting slower all the time
And night don't catch me yawning
Just staring
Just stunned
Starving
And day don't catch me running
Just amazed at the way they used to spell "Ford"

AND SO DOES YOUR MOTHER

I'm tired of this Pop Star Sentimental
Reminiscing on old '40 Fords
And the Beach Boys
And wasn't the Fifties neat
The Fifties sucked dogs man
And so do you
And so does your mother too

ANOTHER TONIGHT

You wake me up with your pale body
And your snake scar
I dreamed of the Great White Shark
And you of tattoos of crashing planes
On the cheek of a Cuban lady
I have to meet a faggot for lunch
But I'll be back for another tonight

LEFT-HANDED KACHINA

In Old Oraibi on the high mesa in Arizona, the oldest settlement in the Western Hemisphere, a Buick pulls up, a tourist and his wife get out and go into a small broken down store and ask about rugs. Old Hopi women with gray braided hair sit around weaving, looking up once then eyes back down. Wikvaya ("one who brings"), a young Hopi, comes into the store and stands in a corner staring at the tourists making them nervous enough to leave. Wikvaya follows them outside and approaches them before they reach the car. He asks them if they want to buy a Kachina doll. They hadn't thought about Kachinas, what they mainly wanted was a rug, but at this point any souvenir of the trip would be good enough. The tourists get in their car expecting to follow Wikvaya in his but instead Wikvaya gets in the front seat right along with them. This is pretty scary for the tourists and exciting at the same time. A real live Indian riding in their car. Wikvaya points out the way and they follow his instructions. Down through small tar paper shacks and huts along a bumpy dirt road. The man would like to carry on some bit of conversation but can't think of anything to say. The woman is concentrating on keeping her right leg from touching Wikvaya's left leg. Wikvaya couldn't care less about any of it. He just stares out at the village with night black eyes. The road twists and turns until it looks like there's no more houses in sight and the man begins to panic. "What if he's taken us out here to murder us? He probably hates white people. After all you can't blame him. All those years of oppression." Then the road runs right up to a small shack with smoke coming out a piece of rusty pipe with wire holding it to the roof. Wikvaya gets out and walks up to the shack. The tourists follow. Conversation in strange broken language mixed with English comes from inside. Wikvaya opens the door and silence falls as the tourists enter the one room. Several young Hopis, some in crew cuts and glasses, one with a transistor radio, one reading an Archie comic book, sit in chairs and on the floor all around the sides of the shack with their backs up against the walls. Corn husks hang from the beams and rafters and one large table filled with Kachina dolls of every size and color and type. A few of the Hopis are whittling softly with jackknives on half-finished kachinas, looking down, eyes not touching the tourists. Wikvaya explains what they've come for and one of them motions to the table. Wikvaya tells the tourists to take their pick. They go to the table and pick up the first one that strikes their eye, anxious to get the hell out of there. They hold up a white one with green stripes. The Hopis shake their heads no, explaining that it's not finished. They hold up another and the same thing happens. Finally they find a black and red one with a bow in the right hand and a rattle in the left. This one they say they can have for fifteen bucks. That seemed a little steep to the tourists but they pay it anyway, not wanting to get into an argument. They say thank you and good bye to Wikvaya then leave with the Kachina tucked under an arm.

Back in New York City the man sets his Kachina on the bookshelf and looks up what type it is in a pamphlet he bought in Phoenix. According to the picture he finds it's called a Left-Handed Kachina but nothing tells about what it represents or what it's for except probably to make rain. He goes out and buys a twenty-dollar record of ancient Hopi chants recorded by the National Archives in the early nineteen-hundreds, brings it home and puts it on the record player. He sits back in his easy chair staring proudly at the Kachina and listening to the ancient drum beat and moaning throb of voices from another time. The Kachina doll suddenly pitches forward off the bookcase, lands on the floor and breaks both arms. The man rushes over and picks it up. His hands begin to sweat. The right hand getting cold and the left one hot. He thinks nothing of it, his big concern is fixing the doll. He finds some epoxy and applies it to the wood, puts the arms back in place and wraps rubber bands around them to hold them firm. He sets the doll back on the bookcase to dry and puts the record back on. By this time he begins to notice his hands more and wipes the sweat off on his pants leg. He closes his eyes and leans back in the chair letting the chant roll over him in waves. In the blackness he sees a long coiling green snake with a horn in its forehead come sliding straight toward him, fangs out and head weaving from side to side. Again the doll falls from the bookcase, both arms snapping loose and sliding across the floor. The man sits straight up, eyes open, fear creeping in. The chant pounds on over and over shifting rhythm and tone. He jumps to his feet and takes the needle off the record but the chant keeps on. He goes to the doll and tries to glue the arms on again but his hands are trembling, sweating. The arms slide from the body to the floor. His right hand is freezing cold, the left hand boiling and the heat creeping all the way up his arm very slow like rattle-snake venom. He finds a rag and makes a tourniquet at the left elbow but his right hand is so cold that the rag keeps slipping from his grip. He pulls at the rag with his teeth then bites down into the veins of his arm. He lets out a low animal moan and finds his voice making the chant. He moves like a dog around the apartment moaning and chanting slashing at his arm. The blood leaves snaking red trails across the carpet. Rain pours from the ceiling soaking, driving hard like needles into his face. Thunder cracks the plaster and lightning slashes through the furniture burning black brands across the walls and floor. Corn springs from the carpet. Rivers gush and spread red earth into all the corners of the apartment. His wife opens the door with an arm load of groceries, accidentally steps on the Kachina and smashes it to bits. Everything stops still. She looks down at the doll then at her husband weeping, moaning, swaying back and forth in a tight ball in the middle of the floor. She drops her load.

RHYTHM

If everything could be sung to the standard rock and roll pro-
gression – C, A minor, F, G chords – then everything'd be simple.
How many variations on a single theme. The greatest drum solo I
ever heard was made by a loose flap of a tarpaulin on top of my
car hitting the wind at eighty. The second best is windshield
wipers in the rain, but more abstract, less animal. Like the
rhythms of a rabbit scratching his chin. Vision rhythms are neat
like hawk swoops and swan dives. Slow motion space rhythms.
Digging rhythms like shovels and spades and hoes and rakes and
snowplow rhythms. Jack-hammer rhythms make Ginger Baker
and Keith Moon look like punk chumps. Oilcan rhythms, ratchet
wrench rhythms. Playing cards in bicycle spokes. A string of
rapid-fire, firecracker rhythms. Propeller rhythms. Cricket
rhythms. Dog claws clicking on hardwood floors. Clocks. Piston
rhythms. Dripping faucets. Tin hitting tin in the wind. Water
slapping rocks. Flesh slapping flesh. Boxing rhythms. Racing
rhythms. Rushing brooks. Radio static buzz in a car when the
engine is the dictator. Directional turnsignal blinkers. Off and on
neon lights. Blinking yellow arrows. Water pumps. Refrigerator
hums. Thermostatic-controlled heating systems. Clicking elevators with the numbers lighting up for each floor. Snakes sliding
through grass. In fact any animal through grass. At night. Buoy
lights. Ship signals. Airplane warnings. Fire alarms. Rhythms in
a stuck car horn. Eating rhythms. Chewing rhythms. The cud of
a cow. The chomp of a horse. Knives being sharpened. Band
saws. Skill saws. Hack saws. Buzz saws. Buck saws. Chain saws.
Any saw rhythm. Hammers and nails. Money clanking in a
poker game. Cards shuffled. Bus meters. Taxi meters. Boiling
water rhythms. Clicking ballpoint pens. Clicking metal frogs.
Roulette wheel spinning rhythms. Tire rhythms. Whittling.
Stitching. Typing. Clicking knitting needles. Parrots sharpening
their beaks on wood. Chickens scratching. Dogs digging for
moles. Birds cleaning their feathers. Cocking guns. Spinning

guns. Bolt actions. Lever actions. Snapping finger nails. Finger popping. Cracking knuckles. Snapping bones. Farting. Spitting. Shitting. Fucking rhythms. Blinking eyes. Blowing nose. Coughing without control. Candle flicker rhythms. Creaking houses. Thawing ice. And you call yourself a drummer?

PEACOCK KILLER

My dog caught a peacock one night and ate it. The next day when I found out I kicked the shit out of him. I broke three of his ribs and cried. Then I found out how dumb peacocks are even though everyone thinks they're beautiful. Shitting on your roof and screaming when they fuck. So I bought a twenty-two and started killing every peacock I could lay my hands on. Me and my dog at night we'd go hunting. I had to use short bullets with a mushroom head so they wouldn't make too much noise. Just like the sound of a small car backfire. Just one shot apiece and if that didn't kill 'em I'd let my dog finish them off. We'd come home bloody and laughing with murder every night. In the mornings the rich neighbors would wake up and find the corpses chewed and blasted up against white picket fences. They hired a private detective to investigate the deaths. Soon it hit the local papers: MAD PEACOCK KILLER ON THE LOOSE. So I changed my tactics. I switched to bow and arrow. I marked each arrow with a special notch and attached a note which read: REVENGE FOR BROKEN RIBS.

LETTER FROM A COLD KILLER

Maybe you'd love me more if I didn't kill for a living
Having to smell my Luger Blackhawk every night
Counting the bullets like my pay check
It's true we move around a lot and it's hard on the kid
You get used to the Dodge and the next day it's gone
At least he gets to see the lay of the land
He loves the trains and the passport changes
What's a lie now and then
The blood on the tie
He's seen that in the movies
Pass it off for lipstick
The powder burned eye
Tell him the matches exploded
Or better yet tell him I'm a Cold Killer
Trying to pay his way through College
And give him a kiss on the head
And tuck him in his bed
And write down what he mumbles in his sky blue sleep

SHARK MOVE

The way a shark can't stop moving or he'll die
That's you on the floor
Sleep swimming on your back
Spitting out your teeth
Sliding like a puck
I can't do nothin' for you 'less you stand up
What you need is a pocket full of crickets
To bring you back to earth

ILLINOIS

Illinois green lush wet dripping corn bacon and tomatoes the size
of your fist fights across the table brother fights father and wife
fights father son fights sister brother fights the priest makes his
visit interrupts the ball game sits down for a meal demanded just
on account of his collar upstairs Jesus bleeds from different positions on the walls crosses nailed to rafters beams and plaster old
radios dixieland drums echo across the barn the Springer Spaniel
has her litter wet and licking milk from straw old hats and halters
paper clippings Truman Roosevelt Churchill trucks rumble the
bridge milk trucks gasoline and apple brandy for the old man wet
wooden porch screen watch the wind go by neighbors picking up
mail crows strut flap leave black feathers on the lawn gravel sing
of high electric wire baseballs rotting in the leaves bats broke and
mitts rubber gloves wires growing through trees and Grandpa
dies in his slippers and Grandpa dies in his baseball cap and
Grandpa dies sitting up.

INSTANT ANIMAL

He was talkin' about the imagery in a good fight
I didn't get it
An outsider no doubt
Him I mean
Talkin' about this guy spilling hot coffee on this other guy
And the good time it was
No stitches
No hospital
No emergency
Just a good yuck
He was talkin' about trust
Measured by action in a life and death move
If someone's there or not there
To be present at death
At the same time in the same place
I'll always trust a dumb guy before a smart one
An instant animal
With no thinking gaps
The gap that kills
The watcher watching the watched
An outsider no doubt
Me I mean

POWER

I can remember racing with my father
The difference in our size and strength
The power in his legs
The quickness in mine
It almost killed him but he won
And afterwards I heard him puke behind the shed
That night I went to bed
And dreamed of power in a train

"CITY OF HOPE"

On the outskirts of Duarte, California, it's dry, flat, cracked and
stripped down. Rock quarries and gravel pits. Trucks roll from
sun to sun. People in the outlying towns call it "Rock Town". The
"City of Hope", an institute dedicated to curing and investigat-
ing the causes of cancer, sits there surrounded by rocks and
cement companies. It provides most of the town with work of
one kind or another. Famous doctors and medical men from all
over the world come to visit and catch up on the latest discover-
ies. A lot of experimenting is done on animals. All kinds of
animals from mice to rats to hamsters to dogs. They're all injected
or fed cancer-causing bacteria and then slowly die and are then
operated on by the famous doctors and then the bodies are
burned in huge incinerators. The smoke and stink of death hangs
over Duarte most of the time. A kid named Jaimie Lee takes care
of the experimental greyhounds. They're kept in a special kennel
house separated from the main building, out in the middle of an
open lot. He arrives each morning at 6.30 sharp in his '51 Chevy,

puts on a long white apron and rubber gloves and boots and gets down to work. There's over twenty-five purebred greyhounds all raised and brought in from Arizona. As soon as one dies there's a new one to take his place the next day. Jaimie has to shift the dogs from their dirty kennels over into clean ones. Then he hoses down the shit and piss and vomit into a gutter. Sometimes on dogs specially marked with yellow or red collars he has to save the shit in a dixie cup and put it in a small ice box for the Japanese doctor to examine later. Then he feeds and waters all the dogs except for certain other specially marked ones who are going to be killed and operated on that day. If he finds a dead dog in the morning he's supposed to call the main office and notify the doctor in charge then wrap the dog in a plastic sheet and place him in a large freezer. Jaimie gets to know each dog personally as they come in and makes up names for them since all they have is numbers when they come. After two or three weeks they start to respond to him like a friend. As soon as they hear his car roll up in the morning, all twenty-five dogs start barking their heads off. He walks down the cement aisle and talks to each one and gives them each a pat on the head. He notices how thin and bony they get after the first week or so and how sleek and healthy they looked when they first came. In the afternoon the doctors come around to give them their injection of poison. There's one favorite dog that Jaimie has that he calls "Swaps". He called him that because one day he let Swaps out for a run in the vacant lot and he couldn't believe how fast and beautiful he was. So he named him after his favorite race horse. It was Swaps' coloring that first attracted Jaimie. A deep red and black brindle color, like a tiger. He found out that Swaps came from a breeder in Arizona who had raised him especially for racing but the dog grew too big so he was shipped to the "City of Hope". Jaimie knew that if he ever got caught letting any of the dogs out for a run that he'd get fired. But he didn't care. Swaps loved to run and Jaimie loved to watch him. He'd always come back when Jaimie whistled and go right into his kennel. Whenever Jaimie took Swaps out all the other dogs would go crazy, barking and howling and throwing themselves against the cyclone fence. On this particular morning Jaimie had finished all the dirty work and went to get Swaps. He swung the gate open and Swaps danced and leaped all around Jaimie and headed straight for the door of the kennel house wagging his tail with joy. Jaimie opened the door and Swaps bolted out like a bullet straight into the morning sunlight. He ran in great circles at top speed, gravel and dirt spitting out from his paws. Jaimie stood in the doorway and watched. What a beautiful wild animal. It got so that Jaimie's vision could slow Swaps' movement down to slow motion like a camera. He could see every muscle move through the shoulders, along the ribs, down through the back legs. The power in every pull and leap. The beautiful tiger stripes flashing across the earth. He wished Swaps would just keep running and never stop, never come back to die. He started to think about Swaps being dead. He saw visions of his corpse in the morning. How he'd have to wrap him up and put him in the freezer. How the Japanese doctor would cut him open with precision and indifference and examine his insides. How he'd have to burn the mutilated body afterwards. The other dogs were barking louder now from inside. Louder than usual it seemed. Every bark nagging at him. Tugging at him. Pulling, demanding. Screaming out for room to run. He turned back inside and looked down the dreary gray cement hallway with the dim electric light bulbs. He went to the first kennel and unlocked it, swung the gate open and a dog he'd named Silky bolted out, went through the open door and blasted into the morning. He went to the next one and opened it. Another one sprung loose and another. On down the whole aisle until all the cages were empty. Just Jaimie Lee standing there alone inside with the smell of wet cement in his nose. He went outside and there was Swaps standing big and regal. The leader of the pack. The rest of them swarming and dancing around him. Jaimie took off his apron, his gloves and his boots and threw them in the dirt. Swaps was watching Jaimie's movements from a distance. Jaimie got in his car and took off down the road. Swaps was hot on his heels with the rest of the pack following along behind. Jaimie looked in his rear view mirror and saw the twenty-five greyhounds stretching out along the highway. He was pacing them at forty miles an hour and they were keeping up. He smiled and turned a right into the main gates with "City of Hope" written in giant letters across the top. Smooth green freshly mowed lawns and immaculately clean white buildings. Nurses wheeling patients in wheel chairs came to a screeching halt to watch the procession. The dogs tore across the lawns, through the corridors, breaking away from the pack then joining it again. Swaps kept the lead the whole time, trying to catch Jaimie's car. Doctors stood open-mouthed, some running for cover. Then Jaimie hung a left and headed up the road toward the Safeway Shopping Center. Then he hit the Bank, the Post Office, the Library and the Park. The dogs never seemed to tire. They couldn't get enough of it. He headed straight out toward Azusa. Then Cucamunga and Upland and the grape vineyards. It was there he lost them. All except for Swaps whom he kept for a friend.

YOUR JUICE

Wicked
Tasty
Red
And ripe
To touch
To have
In hand
The juice
Of you

MOON PRAYER

Sacred
Night
Moon
Sacred
Light
New
Like a man
Precious
Time
Precious
Few
Worship the animal
The animal
You

ARSON

You have to go on your belly for a long way, then half standing, then crawling on all fours under alders, then walking up to your knees almost in standing algae water that smells like rotten wood. Sometimes you can skirt the impossible passages by going up the shaggy sides of the mountain and around the spruce trees watching out for dead porky pines 'cause they still got their quills and if you get stuck by one they just work their way in deeper and deeper. Finally you get to a place where different kinds of sycamores grow. Don't ask me how they got in the same place with spruce and alders, but they're there. The area up there opens out more and there's room to move around in. You start collecting dry twigs, sunburned leaves and the shaggy bark from the sycamore. Birch bark is best. Then you build all these up in a pile in a dry brushy place close to dead trees and small bushes and in the open enough to catch the wind. Then take a long book of paper matches like the kind they give out in fancy hotels and tie a long piece of white string soaked in kerosene to the match book. Place the book of matches in the middle of the pile of kindling and light the string, then run. Find an open fire-path back that runs in the opposite direction of the wind. Once you get down the mountain find a high tree well covered with leaves and climb it. Sit there all night and watch the beautiful orange glow eat up the blackness and listen to the far away snapping and booms as trees explode and fall like planes shot down and smell the blue smoke cut through the mountain air and pinch at your nose like a starving man cut off from a barbecue.

THE SEX OF FISHES

They were talking about the corniness of the word "slice". Then she said an even cornier one was "portion". What kind of people use the word "portion"? Then that got 'em laughing for a while. They were waiting for company. In the mean time he loaded up the .22 with longs and went out to squeeze off some crows. Five times he missed but they left the garden alone after that. The goat didn't like the shots too much and began dancing on her hind legs, her udder slapping from side to side. As he took the bolt out of the gun and set it in the cupboard he was thinking of his mother. How she was coming to visit and probably make comments on the length of the baby's hair. "Boy or girl? Boy or girl?" He looked at his woman as he re-loaded the clip with five more shells. She looked like a little boy doing the dishes. His hands looked long and slender like a woman's. The gun looked male through and through. The deer were female, even the bucks. Porcupines, little fat boys. Ducks – chicks. Moose – men. Fox – female. Wolves – a little of both. Rabbit – girl fuzzies. Fish? He couldn't place. A fish is a hard one to place. Fish are definitely mysterious. With that he packed it in for the night.

SEA SLEEP

The bed was an ocean to him even when he was awake. The blankets swirled like the waves. The sheets crashed like the white caps. Seagulls dove down and fished along his back. He hadn't been up for days and the people in the house were getting worried. He wouldn't talk or eat. Just sleep and wake and fall asleep again. When they called the doctor he pissed all over him. When they called a psychiatrist he spit. When they called a priest he puked. Finally they let him be and just slid carrots and lettuce under the door. These were the only things he'd eat. The people in the house started a joke about their pet rabbit and he overheard it. His hearing was getting very keen. So he stopped eating altogether. He slid the bed in front of the door so no one could get in and then fell fast asleep. At night the people would hear hurricane sounds coming from the room. Thunder and lightning and foghorns. They banged on the door. They tried to break it down but the door held firm. They put their ears to the door and heard gurgling underwater sounds. Moss and barnacles started to grow on the outside walls of the room. The people were afraid. They decided to have him committed but when they went to get their car they discovered the house surrounded by ocean on all sides as far as they could see. Nothing but ocean. The house tossed and heaved all night. The people huddled together in the basement. From up in the room came a long low moan and the whole house sank into the sea.

CLEAN GREEN

Seventy-five fathoms
Down
Six feet to the fathom
Six miles
Out
Drunk to a rip tide
Snared by a rock rope
Dragged to the deep blue
Bottom
Bones unseen
Just the clean green table top
Waiting for the next pool shark
To come play fish

SNAKE TIDE

Snake tide
Sneaky
Green
Foam break
Slips up
Back
And soaks the dry
Thirsty earth's
Cracked cry
Of longing to be out there
Moving
With the sea green sea

RUNNING OUT OF TROUBLE (1964)

I kept having these particular little thought schemes that kept happening more and more. At first they wouldn't take up too much of my attention and I'd notice them more after they'd happened than at the instant I was involved. Then it came about that all I was having all the time were these particular little thought schemes around one particular theme. I'd be some-where in a house with several rooms and all I was thinking each time I went into a new room was how each room would be to live in if I were sentenced to life imprisonment. The thought of being sentenced or who was doing the sentencing or why didn't matter at all. All my particular little thought schemes were concerned with was how to survive in this or that particular room with whatever the room had to offer. If the room had a lot to offer like a fireplace I'd start thinking about wood and digging the wood supply and calculating how long it would last before I'd have to forget about wood and the fireplace and go on to something else like family portraits and family seals and crests and coats of arms. I figured that interest in them articles would last only so long and no longer so I'd hunt around for new stuff to dazzle and titillate like ashtrays made out of milk glass and photographs of the Civil War and a glass table with a glass bowl in the middle filled with glass grapes and glass pears. Then I'd start thinking about food and being fed and eating and quickly decided that I should check out the kitchen and see what sort of prison that would make. I'd be fed there at least but then sooner or later I'd run into the same trouble I had with the wood. Running-out trouble. Then I began to see that running-out trouble was real trouble and it was the kind of trouble I was running up against all the time and that these particular little thought schemes weren't just hypothetical and all. These particular little thought schemes were really involved in trying to work something out that was happening right there at the time they were going on and not just preparing for something to come. So I ran out the front door and on to the lawn which is green and smooth and serene as Pennsylvania and I yell as loud as all get out that I was in real trouble on account of all I had was glass grapes and a short supply of wood and right next door a short, bald, fat, cigar-in-hand gentleman in red leather slippers walks on to the porch and saunters over to my side of the fence and wraps his fat cigar hand around my neck and says to me not to worry 'cause help was on the way and sure enough a pickup truck stops in front of the lawn and a short fat guy with baseball cap gets out with an armful a wood.

ELECTRIC FOG

O'Neill
Fog
Electric
Light
Jaimie
Morphine
Sea
Fog
Electric
North
East
Coast
Sad
Electric
Night

BATTLE LACE

Welts
Bleeding loud
From belting
With buckles
And lace
Across her face
She sure smarts now
Kept by compadres
In battle halls

College dorms and
Mounted cannon
On the peak roofs
Scanning football fields
Like movies
Like life copying movies
Like flesh and blood
Still she sticks around
For lack of another place
To go to

THE MOVEMENT OF STOPPING

I'll sit in one place. It could come about from what I've done before. You know, walking along and just coming to a stop somewhere. Just stopping.

Don't you want to go?

Just stopped. Everything drags you down. There's a collection of junk in your throat, in your chest. Your blood hardens up. I'm standing there and a silver Mercedes Benz comes along and stops right beside me for no special reason except that the light is red. I'm stopped. I stare through their window. I see them surrounded in leather. Leather seats, leather roof, leather clothes. If they moved one inch everything would squeak. They haven't moved hardly at all because of the squeaky leather. Their radio's on. James Brown is screaming to go back to school in his leather pants. She lays her hand in his lap. They stare straight out the window. The light turns green but his joint is getting hard and the leather bulges up. She sees me and smiles. She squeezes his prick. He turns the channel. Little Stevie Wonder is singing about a place in the sun. A guy starts wiping their window with a bloody rag. He grabs the gear shift and rubs up and down. The light changes red. This is really happening. I could go somewhere else.

Why don't you?

I move down the block and begin to stop again. Again I'm stopped. I'm standing there and thinking all about High School. The movement of High School. A cement slab on the Mojave Desert which is architecturally magnificent. A place to bake your feet. A block with circles and incest in the faculty. A little teacher with a baby face getting sucked by the Fine Arts lady. I'm moving out in the world. Look at me move Ma.

Why don't you move?

ROLLING RENAULT

Teddy? Well I can tell you when it was the last time I saw Teddy. He was driving a 1951 green Renault at the time and came by to pick me up. I'd been waiting underneath a billboard sign advertising Ford when he slid into it and I got in. Right away I realized the slide was something peculiar to Teddy's usual method of handling Renaults and I began to question his technique when lo and behold I see a brown paper bag on the back seat and ask him what it's about. Teddy tells me to see for myself and I reach my hand back there and peek in the bag and lo and behold I catch sight of more dexedrine and bennies then I ever saw in my life. Well I turn slowly around and don't say a word. We've been driving for some while now when I notice Teddy ain't stopping for a thing. I begin talking to him, hoping that speaking will bring him down some. I ask him what he's stolen lately at the factory and he tells me it's not a factory but a specialized corporation with branches around the world. I ask him then how he's feeling lately about his job and he asks me how I would feel if I made invisible circuits for future installation in a bigger camera to film the nose cone of Gemini 7 as it turns back toward earth. I see he's in another world and I'm about to turn on WABC when Teddy sees about four miles up the road a 1948 Chrysler sedan slowly pulling across the road. He whips the wheel to the left and the left front wheel hits the curb and the axle breaks and the car hits a lamp post and flips over and rolls four times landing right side up in a gas station with the top crushed and all the glass smashed except for the front window which popped out somewhere on the grass.

THE ESCAPES OF BUSTER KEATON

If you ever have a mind to, what you can do some time instead of what you usually do is turn on the old TV and turn down the sound so you can't hear the words and just watch the funny picture. You could also do the reverse of that and turn on the old TV and fuck up the picture so it's not a picture and only waves and dots and lights moving up and down and in and out and turn the sound way up. Then you can take part in narrating an escape. If you notice the escapes of Buster Keaton you're bound to learn something. You learn first of all that you don't have to try. You see him in action and you notice it's a double action with two opposites happening simultaneously. You notice the face just being a face and nothing more or less than a face and for that reason it becomes more of a face but don't worry. You notice the body performing more things than a body can perform and being sometimes more than a body and sometimes less and for that reason becoming something more than a body. You see the face not worried about the body and the body not worried about the face and then he escapes. You're trapped watching while he escapes. The thing that strikes you most is that he doesn't worry about being caught.

VOICES FROM THE DEAD
(Monologues written for the Open Theatre, 1969)

COWBOY: The Rodeo Association made the Suicide Grip illegal in somethin' like 1959 but that didn't stop no bull rider I knew from usin' the damn thing. First off you take the glove on your grip hand and pull the fingers loose by about three-quarters of an inch and wrap them around the rigging so it's like the glove is tied down with your hand stuck inside. Then you pound yer fist shut on the rope with yer free hand 'til you stop the blood from runnin'. When that chute opens boy you hang on like epoxy to wood. This bull I drew was called The Twister and boy he did just that. Circles. Like he was dancin' on a dime. Didn't even have time to mark him once before he had me up against the fence. Never knew eight seconds could be so long. A cowboy knows when he's got a good ride. Soon as he comes out he knows. If it's good he don't even listen for no bell he just rides. If it's good everything's in one place. You just flap with the bucks like you was an extra piece a skin on that bull's back. If it's bad he's got you all crooked and prayin' for balance. Achin' for the bell. This time I knew I was hurtin'. He kept slammin' my legs up against that damn fence and each time I heard a board crack I heard a bone to go along with it. I saw the whole arena zigzagging like a roller coaster ride. The ten-gallon hats and American flags. That bullhorn squawkin' about Levis and popcorn and ferris wheels and "Here comes Billie Joe Brody from Thunder Creek, South Dakota on The Twister! Look at this boy ride. Watch out there! Watch out Billie Joe!" Then he had me sideways. My whole body snapped clean across his back. All except that hand. That grip hand stuck in there for dear life. First thing I thought was, "Now they know I'm a cheater. Now they know. They can all see my glove stuck underneath that riggin' rope. Coast-to-coast TV. Mom and Pop back in Thunder Creek. Down at the bar. Only TV in the whole damn town. Now they know." I felt it come loose at the shoulder. Right where the ball fits into the socket. A cowboy gets to know about anatomy after all them years. Nothin' but flesh and muscle holdin' me on to that bull now. He keeps whippin' me around like a dish towel or somethin'. Slam into that fence. Slam! Somethin' breaks loose. All blood and strings comin' out. All I want is to be free a them hooves. Down he comes straight on my back. Everything breaks. I can feel it. Like my whole insides is made a glass. Everything splinters and shatters. I see the face a the clown. He's got a terror mask on. Usually calm and cool as you please. Now he's wavin' that bandana like an old fish wife chasin' off the neighbors' kids. That bull don't move from me once. Not one inch. He's mad. Mad at me. Mad as all hell and he ain't lettin' me go. Not never. He's got me this time and he knows it. I ain't never gonna get up again. He's makin' me part a the earth. Mashin' me down. Pulverizin' my flesh. Sendin' me back where I come from. Then he's gone. Straight at the crowd, all screamin' and yellin'. Half fear, half ecstasy. They got more than a buck's worth this time out. The gates open on the far end of the arena and I can see this Cadillac comin'. A big black car. Can't tell if it's a hearse or an ambulance. Don't much give a damn. The ground tastes like earth.

STONE MAN: I'm stone. "The Living Stone Man". They call me that. They did. At Pacific Ocean Park. They brought me from Malaysia. They found me like that. Just lying there straight out, stiff. Stiff as a board. "The Living Stiff." Right past the cotton-candy machine that spins pink stuff around an aluminum disc. That's where you could have bought a ticket. They have me in a house trailer. The same kind they have on display with butane double-burner stoves and fold-out, tuckaway beds. This one has my pictures outside. Black-and-white snapshots showing me in different positions of stiffness. One where I'm laying straight out horizontal on a chair. Like levitation except there's a chair there. In fact they sometimes display me that way. Only my eyes move. That's how they know I'm alive. They feed me with a tube. Milk, soup, egg yolks, stuff like that. They hand out hat pins at the door of the trailer for anyone who doesn't believe that I'm really "The Petrified Man". They stick me sometimes but most of the time they get too afraid. They see my eyes moving, looking at them. They get too afraid. One day my eyes stopped moving but they kept me on display anyway. They kept sticking me with needles. In fact more people stuck me with needles now because my eyes stopped moving. I could still feel the needles even though my eyes stopped.

TELEPORTED MAN: I was trying to get to China. My atoms were to be decomposed in New York and recomposed in Hong Kong. They said there was nothing to fear. It had worked hundreds of times before without an accident. I'd saved for five years for this trip. Five years. They had me take off my clothes and enter the tube. I had to lie straight out horizontal with my head up, strapped into the electronic beamer. My legs and arms strapped, my back rigid. I looked straight ahead to the end of the tube or what seemed to be the end. A spiral of light going out and out. Yellow light like the halos you see on Jesus in all the paint-ings. The sides of the tube glistened and shined, sending off waves of light, like steam heat except it was light. A sound traveled down the tube from the top to the bottom. A line of green light. I'd never seen sound before. It weaved and bobbed as though it were looking for me, like a thin green snake with its tongue spitting. It found me. The top of my head then right in the center of my forehead, like a third eye burrowing in. It felt like an eye at least. A new sight. I could see with my brain. My whole head lit up with the sound. My body became the sound. Pulsing to the vibrations. All the way down my spine and into my rectum. I could feel myself going away. The body. I didn't look down to see because I wasn't afraid. I knew it would work. The epidermis, the tissue, the muscle fibre, the veins, and blood, the bones, the heart, intestines. Each piece growing away from me until there I was, left alone. Hanging in mid-air like a ghost. Just my spirit, my brain, no not my brain but something that knew I was there even though I wasn't, in the flesh. I started to move up the tube. Moving through space in a vacuum. Something seemed to pull me along. I was shot out the tube and into space. I could see boats pulling away from the harbor and planes taking off. I was moving at a tremendous rate. I never felt so light and free. Like I was part of the air. Lighter than air. Land vanished and everything below me was water then clouds then high above. I couldn't tell how fast I was going now. Everything seemed timeless and space opened out and out. I'd never felt so free in my life. Then suddenly I couldn't get back. I couldn't go on and I couldn't go back. I knew I was lost. I reached out for my body, for something hard and real. My legs, my arms. Anything. The panic filled me. I was going to die in mid-air. Out of my body. Somewhere in space between New York and Hong Kong. I was being pulled toward the stars. Deeper and deeper in space. I searched for my voice but nothing was there. I tried to scream and nothing came out. No one was there to hear me or see me. I was absolutely alone. I longed to be human again. To crash to the earth and die like a man.

HOW LONELY CAN IT GET IN A HOLE?

The bottom fell out. There was no way up to the top. Even the light at the top was black. An endless pit. Stork Clark heard the cars roar by and asked the little boy holding his hand and leading the way, "Why don't they turn their lights on? They can see I'm out here." The little boy didn't answer, afraid to embarrass his blindness. "How lonely can it get in a hole?" the little boy asked. Stork Clark didn't answer. He was driving a team of horses through the timber with a load of coffee for the lumberjacks. "I'm not afraid of the dark," the little boy said. "Well you oughta be," said Stork. All through the village they whispered, "Poor old devil." A silent whisper which Stork understood to be night. "Maybe it's an eclipse. I've seen it get like this up in the Yukon." The boy didn't understand the word "eclipse" but took it to mean a circle. "We've been walking straight North."

"I know my way around kid. I grew up in these woods. Don't forget that. The sun should be comin' before too long. I've seen it like this in the North." He pulled at the boy's hand and took the lead, straining with his head forward like a draft horse. "You oughta let me lead ya Stork. There's a lot a trucks out tonight." Stork broke to the left and broke loose from the boy's grip, walking straight out into the fields toward the woods. The kid ran after him yelling, "Hey! They want me to bring you back for supper Stork! Hey!" Stork kept walking strong stumbling on old plow ruts and plodding on. The kid kept chasing him, pulling at his arm. Stork growled and shoved him away. "I'll find my way out. You tell 'em that. I'll find my way." "But you're heading straight for the woods!"

Stork slipped between a line of blue spruce trees and disappeared. The boy was afraid to go in after him and afraid to go back to the Rest Home and tell them he'd lost the old man. He sat down and listened to the crunching snapping footsteps of Stork fade off and go silent. He cried for a while and looked at the moon. He felt the silent secret night coming in and watched the headlights of lumber trucks shake down the road, far off. He watched all the houses and the lights inside. The difference between the outside and the inside. He imagined all the people sitting inside. Warm. Talking. Reading. Knitting. Smoking. Drinking coffee and tea. He got up and walked back through the field to the road. He flagged down a big truck and climbed aboard. "Where to?" the driver asked. The kid just stared. "How lonely can it get in a hole?" he thought.